MINIATURE ROOMS

THE THORNE ROOMS AT THE ART INSTITUTE OF CHICAGO

MINIATURE ROOMS

THE THORNE ROOMS AT THE ART INSTITUTE OF CHICAGO

THE ART INSTITUTE OF CHICAGO

ABBEVILLE PRESS · PUBLISHERS
NEW YORK · LONDON · PARIS

All color photography in this book, except for the portrait of Mrs. Thorne in her studio on page 8, is the work of Kathleen Culbert-Aguilar and Michael Abramson. All black and white illustrations are taken from The Art Institute of Chicago's Thorne Room files, except for that on page 25, which is by Culbert-Abramson.

Front cover illustration: English Dining Room of the Georgian Period, 1770–90 (E-10).

Back cover illustration: Tennessee Entrance Hall, 1835 (A-31), in which a long-stemmed rose has been placed to provide a sense of scale. The room measures 14⅛ x 14½ x 30¼ inches.

Frontispiece: French Bedroom, late 16th century (E-17).

The book was designed by Harvey Retzloff, Chicago, Illinois.

The book was printed by Toppan Printing Co., Ltd., Japan.

Library of Congress Cataloging in Publication Data
Art Institute of Chicago.
    The Thorne miniature rooms, the Art Institute
of Chicago.
    1. Miniature rooms—Illinois—Chicago.   2. Thorne,
James Ward, Mrs.—Art collections.   3. Miniature
rooms—Private collections—Illinois—Chicago.
4. Art Institute of Chicago.   I. Weingartner, Fannia.
II. Title.
NK2117.M54A7   1984   747′.0228   83-8788
ISBN 0-89659-407-6
ISBN 0-89659-408-4 (pbk.)

15   14   13   12   11   10   9   8   7

Contents

PREFACE AND ACKNOWLEDGMENTS   7

CREATING THE THORNE ROOMS   *by Bruce Hatton Boyer*   9

THE THORNE ROOMS   *Entries compiled by Fannia Weingartner*
Photographs by Kathleen Culbert-Aguilar and Michael Abramson

EUROPEAN ROOMS   27

AMERICAN ROOMS   91

GLOSSARY OF SELECTED TERMS   167

Preface and Acknowledgments

The continuing popularity of the Thorne Miniature Rooms at The Art Institute of Chicago and repeated requests for a book with color illustrations led to the decision to produce a new account of the rooms in one volume with two full-color illustrations for each of the 68 models. Chicago photographers Kathleen Culbert-Aguilar and Michael Abramson devoted endless hours and painstaking care to achieve the record of the rooms that appears in the following pages. To capture the soft, indirect lighting of the rooms, the photographers made exposures that took as long as 15 minutes.

Since the text of the previous Thorne Rooms books was written some 40 years ago by Meyric B. Rogers, Curator of Decorative Arts at the Art Institute, it seemed appropriate to prepare a new text incorporating more current terminology and information. To provide the kind of perspective that is possible only after the passage of time, Chicago writer Bruce Hatton Boyer was asked to prepare an introduction on the tradition of miniatures and on Mrs. Thorne's method of creating these rooms. Fannia Weingartner, a Chicago-based writer and editor of historical materials, compiled the texts on each of the 68 rooms. Her wide-ranging responsibilities on this project included research, writing, re-writing, and coordinating the project with the Art Institute's Publications Department. In preparing the entries for the European Rooms, Weingartner

These items, drawn from the European miniature rooms, are pictured in their actual sizes based on a scale of one inch to a foot. The sofa and rug are from Room E-28; the easel from E-7; the tall case clock from E-4; and the harp from E-26.

introduced excerpts from Mrs. Thorne's informal notes, which add considerable insight into the reasons for her choice of rooms and furnishings. In the case of the American Rooms, for which there were no such notes, extensive use was made of material from the brochures and handbooks available for some of the historic homes that inspired several interiors and of various reference works.

All of the entries were reviewed by Lynn Springer Roberts, Curator of European Decorative Arts at the Art Institute. Theodore Dell of New York reviewed the text for the French rooms. Anne F. Woodhouse, Curator of Decorative Arts at the State Historical Society of Wisconsin, reviewed entries for the American rooms. The unique familiarity of Alice Pirie Hargrave, Technical Assistant for the Thorne Rooms, with the models and the archival materials related to them gave her a key role in every stage of the project. Mrs. Thorne's son Niblack and his wife Suzanne offered important information for the introduction.

Susan F. Rossen, Editor and Coordinator of Publications at the Art Institute, served as editor. Cris Ligenza, Editorial Secretary in the Publications Department, typed the manuscript and attended to many of the details involved in the production of this work. The glossary that appears at the end of the book was prepared by Betty Seid, Publications Department Assistant, who did other research as well. The book was designed by Harvey Retzloff of Chicago.

Mrs. James Ward Thorne (1882–1966) working in her studio, Chicago, Illinois, 1960.

Creating the Thorne Rooms

BRUCE HATTON BOYER

The Thorne Miniature Rooms are one of the most beloved exhibits at The Art Institute of Chicago. Each year thousands of visitors travel slowly down the long, darkened Thorne galleries in ones and twos, peering into the 68 lighted boxes which transport their imaginations to far-off times and places. For many of them, the Thorne Rooms are the most unusual exhibit in the museum. Although the Thorne Rooms are now close to 50 years old, their appeal seems as fresh as ever. Why have they remained so popular?

The answer probably has to do with the fact that they are miniatures. There is something universally fascinating and magical about miniatures which accounts for their continued use over the centuries. The Egyptians, for example, buried their dead with clay representations of everything the deceased might need in the afterlife: tools, animals, furniture, and servants. In the Orient, home shrines served as miniaturizations of temple statuary. In the West, during medieval times, the Virgin Mary and patron saints were often miniaturized as talismans, and from the 13th century to the present, Christmas celebrations have included the depiction of the Nativity through elaborate crêche scenes. As long as there have been ships, sailors have carved scrimshaw miniatures during long voyages. It is in fact impossible to contemplate the history of art and icon without coming upon every kind of miniature.

On a more familiar level, miniatures evoke our childhoods. Nearly all of us played with some form of miniature as children, whether with dolls, toy soldiers, model railroads, or a tiny stove and dishes like the ones our mothers used. Yet it will not do, if we are to assess properly the achievement of Mrs. Thorne and her craftsmen, simply to say that "the Thorne Rooms bring out the child in us" and leave it at that. The experience of the Thorne Rooms is more complex.

For in addition to reminding us of childhood, the Thorne Rooms are themselves an historic exhibit. Although they do depict highlights from the history of architecture, interior design, and the decorative arts between 1600 and 1940, they reflect something else as well. In the years since the rooms' creation, further scholarship has refined and expanded our ideas about the history of European and American interior design. Looking at the rooms today, we can see that they reveal not only Mrs. Thorne's personal vision but one that is deeply rooted in the ideas and conventions of her time.

It is important not to underestimate the appeal of the workmanship displayed in the Thorne Rooms. The detail in each room is invariably astonishing, the delicacy of execution exquisite. "How did they do that?" is a question heard over and over in the gallery. Most of us can only guess at the hours of painstaking labor that went into each room, not to mention the furniture and marvelously wrought accessories. We literally cannot believe what we are looking at, so complete are the illusions.

Perhaps some knowledge of Mrs. Thorne's background, plus a glimpse of how the rooms were actually constructed, can help us appreciate what makes the Thorne Rooms so appealing.

* * *

Mrs. James Ward Thorne was an amateur in the true sense of that word. She had no formal training in architecture, interior design, or the visual arts. Yet through the creation of close to one hundred rooms over a ten-year period, she managed to set what has become the world standard for workmanship and detail in miniature display.

The word "amateur" has come into some disrepute in recent years. It is often used today to imply incompetence or awkwardness. In an era of computers, advanced degrees, and trips to the moon, the notion prevails that something done by an amateur just cannot, somehow, be good. However, the idea of the gifted amateur has a long and honored tradition in Western society. Leonardo da Vinci, a painter by trade, was a most talented amateur inventor and anatomist. Thomas Jefferson, trained as a statesman, was the gifted amateur architect of Monticello and the University of Virginia. Benjamin Franklin, who always listed his trade as printer, invented the stove that bears his name and helped write the Constitution.

The word "amateur" comes from the Latin *amare,* to love. An amateur, simply put, is one who pursues an activity for love rather than for money. And love is what Mrs. Thorne lavished upon her work. A member by marriage of an important Chicago family, she devoted many years of her life and considerable portions of her substantial financial resources to the creation of her beloved rooms. What she lacked in formal artistic training she made up for with diligence, aptitude, and a keen sense of mission. It was her passion, combined with a unique confluence of historic and economic opportunities, that made the Thorne Rooms a reality.

Born Narcissa Niblack in Vincennes, Indiana, in 1882, she was the daughter of a prominent businessman. Her

Mrs. Thorne with her two sons, Niblack and Ward, outside the family residence in Lake Forest, Illinois, 1917.

Mrs. Thorne, c. 1915.

early schooling was at the hands of a governess. At the age of 11 she was sent to public school and, subsequently, to a private school. Looking back in later years, she commented somewhat wistfully, "The trouble with my childhood was that I was given no education. Knowing how to put my hat on straight was supposed to be enough."

True, it was not much of an education by modern standards, but by the standards of the day it was not uncommon. The world was a far smaller and more intimate place at the turn of the century than it is today. London and Paris were the capitals of gracious society; Boston, Washington, and Philadelphia were their American counterparts. Any young lady "of means" was expected to absorb the manners of these places and not pay much attention to anything else.

Narcissa Niblack absorbed her lessons well. She accompanied her family on their travels to the East Coast and to Europe. Her sparse education was augmented considerably by tours of castles and fine country homes on both sides of the Atlantic. When her family moved to Chicago, sometime before 1900, she saw even more.

In 1901 she married James Ward Thorne, whom she had known since childhood. He was the son of George R. Thorne, co-founder of Montgomery Ward and Company with A. Montgomery Ward. James and his three brothers all worked for the company. A vice-president and director, James retired in 1926 at the age of 53, enabling him to travel extensively with his wife.

By the time she married, Narcissa Niblack had achieved all the success to which a young lady of her background could aspire. She was beautiful, gracious, and well-liked. By all accounts, she was delightful company—warm and open-hearted. Her marriage to James Ward Thorne gave her both wealth and social connections. It is no surprise that she quickly became prominent in Chicago society, giving her time to cultural institutions like The Art Institute of Chicago and the Chicago Historical Society, and to various charities like the Woman's Exchange and several hospitals. The Thornes had two sons, Ward and Niblack. The couple continued to travel, and she continued to indulge in her childhood passion: collecting miniatures.

Her son Niblack recalls his mother's explanation of her lifelong fascination with miniatures as a compulsion; when she saw one, she just had to have it. A variety of reasons probably contributed to her love of miniatures. Certainly, dollhouses and toy soldiers were a common feature of childhood in her day. We do know that she was quite fond of dollhouses; in later years she recalled with affection one particular dollhouse with which she had played during her first years in Chicago. We also know that her uncle Rear Admiral Albert P. Niblack sent her miniatures that he picked up in his travels around the world. Many people have similar experiences without going further, but Mrs. Thorne was able to convert this childhood pastime into a lifetime work that would entertain and educate millions.

During the 1920s, and especially after Mr. Thorne's retirement, the Thornes spent much time abroad. The world they saw on these trips was quite different from that in which they had grown up. World War I had seen to that. The great empires had been shattered. The supremacy of England and France in matters of art, manners, and taste was on the decline. The new powers of Russia and China had emerged as the result of violent revolutions. New styles of art had burst onto the scene as well—Cubism, Expressionism, and Surrealism—styles that were quite divorced from the grand and genteel traditions of earlier centuries.

With these social and cultural upheavals came opportunities. The shifting economic order left many a once-wealthy family in need of money. Precious artifacts, including miniatures which had once graced elegant dollhouses and private collections in Europe, came onto the market at prices undreamed of ten years earlier. Mrs. Thorne was not one to let such opportunities pass. By 1930 the Thornes' apartment on North Lake Shore Drive in Chicago was so overflowing with miniatures that she rented a studio on Oak Street, a few blocks away, to relieve the crush.

It was sometime during the 1920s that Mrs. Thorne conceived the idea of creating miniature rooms. There are several stories about just how the idea came to her, including one that traces it to her discovery of a miniature shadow box in a bazaar in Istanbul. But there were other important influences as well.

The single most important catalyst was the appearance in American museums of full-scale period rooms. The idea of the period room—one that is carefully fashioned to re-create a real or imagined room from a bygone era—had been around for a half-century. The Essex Institute in Salem, Massachusetts, is generally credited with being the first American museum to install period rooms, which it did as early as 1907. By the 1920s the idea caught fire. In 1924 The Metropolitan Museum of Art in New York opened its collection of period rooms, spanning four centuries. The Art Institute of Chicago, The Detroit Institute of Arts, and The Brooklyn Museum followed suit in short order. It was during the 1920s also that the Rockefeller family undertook the restoration of Colonial Williamsburg.

The period room, and by extension, the period village, was intended to serve an educational purpose. Mrs. Thorne, with her long years of volunteer work at major cultural institutions, found the concept appealing. She also saw that the creation of enough full-sized rooms to offer anything approaching a comprehensive look at European and American interior design would require more space than any museum could possibly spare. Constructing such rooms in miniature was a perfect way to solve the problem.

In choosing this method, Mrs. Thorne was following another tradition of long standing: the royal dollhouse. Because the royal dollhouse had quite a different purpose from its present-day counterpart, it is worth a brief examination. An invention of the 16th century, it was intended to serve as a three-dimensional catalogue of its owner's possessions, a testimony to his greatness, wealth, and position. Duke Albert V of Bavaria, whose Baby House of 1558 is generally regarded as the first royal dollhouse, commissioned several such elaborate structures to display tiny replicas of his belongings. Throughout the 16th and 17th centuries, other such dollhouses were built by teams of craftsmen for nobles and wealthy burghers alike. The value placed on such houses was closely related to the intricacy of the workmanship.

The vital difference between royal dollhouses and modern ones is that the royal versions were never intended to be playthings for children. Indeed, the very idea of "play-ing" with a dollhouse was completely absent. Instead, children were encouraged to view the houses as examples of proper living; it was assumed that they would absorb the "lessons" in decorum and manners that such houses displayed. Thus, royal dollhouses were instruments of instruction rather than sources of amusement. One of the most recent examples, still on display today at Windsor Castle, was Queen Mary's Dollhouse, created during the 1920s. Its elaborate workmanship and exquisite detail certainly provided some inspiration for Mrs. Thorne.

A third phenomenon that influenced the creation of the Thorne Rooms was the growing fashion among wealthy Americans during the early decades of this century, and in the 1920s in particular, for building and furnishing their residences in various historical styles. By the 1930s, the way of life exemplified by the elegant estates of England, France, Germany, and what had been the Austro-Hungarian Empire was rapidly disappearing. The displacement of the old by the new appears to have made many of the well-to-do all the more nostalgic for the styles and manners of the pre-World War I era. The most emulated period was the 18th century, both in England and in France. The great appeal of the art, architecture, and decorative arts of this particular epoch for these Americans seems to have been its comfortable elegance, aristocratic associations, and compatibility with their gracious way of life. But homes or rooms of other periods—Tudor or French Renaissance, for example—were also frequently designed. Among the most spectacular and best known homes built in this historicizing spirit are Henry E. Huntington's San Marino in California, James Deering's Vizcaya in Florida, and, most notably, William Randolph Hearst's San Simeon, also in California. It should be noted that innumerable city apartments and suburban homes were designed and decorated in this taste, as well.

Some of these environments incorporated genuine articles imported from Europe, sometimes even whole rooms. Dealers like Sir Joseph Duveen scoured Europe and Russia for his clients to find authentic paintings and sculpture, furniture, porcelain, and other objects. Most interiors, however, were pure pastiches, approximating the look of the period being imitated. Interior decorating firms like P. W. French of New York and Alavoine of New York and Paris were hired to design and produce paneling, furniture, draperies, upholstery, and carpets, which they then arranged and maintained; they were even asked to purchase appropriate silver, crystal, dishware, and linens. Understandably, the creation of such ambitious and expensive decorating projects slowed down considerably after the Depression and all but ceased after World War II.

* * *

It was the confluence of all these social, economic, and cultural factors that gave Mrs. Thorne a rare chance to turn her private hobby into an extraordinary public display. She plunged into the creation of her rooms with the same

Mrs. Thorne posing before a Louis XVI bedroom during an exhibition of her first set of miniature rooms in the early 1930s.

passion that had marked her collecting. Her son Niblack recalls that she went to the studio nearly every day, often for long hours, and that at times there were 30 rooms in various stages of completion in her tiny studio quarters. Often there were several craftsmen at work in the studio at the same time—one creating architectural shells, another doing plasterwork, while a third carved the miniature moldings.

In 1932 the first set of Thorne Rooms—30 in all—was put on display at the Chicago Historical Society for a benefit for the Architectural Students' League. One year later, the same thirty rooms were displayed to a much larger audience when they were installed in their own special building at Chicago's Century of Progress Exposition. Hundreds of thousands of people lined up to see them. Much encouraged by the popularity and success of the rooms, Mrs. Thorne began work on a new and even grander project.

In the first set of rooms Mrs. Thorne for the most part had used miniatures that she already owned, so that the contents of her collection had in large measure dictated the historic periods she depicted. For this new set of rooms Mrs. Thorne fixed upon a comprehensive approach. She decided to follow a chronological scheme, and so to present a history of European design, creating the furniture and accessories from scratch where necessary. This enabled her to maintain a consistent scale of one inch to the foot in every room from this point on, except for the interior of the church Our Lady Queen of Angels (E-29). Mrs. Thorne has been credited with establishing one of the standard proportions used by miniaturists.

The design and construction of this second set of rooms occupied her until 1937. She went to Europe several times expressly to collect miniatures and to study rooms she might wish to copy. Her husband accompanied her and, since he was a dedicated amateur photographer, no doubt helped her in her research by photographing the homes they visited.

Mrs. Thorne had all of Europe to choose from, which makes her final choice of rooms quite interesting. (The Chinese and Japanese rooms appear to have been added as

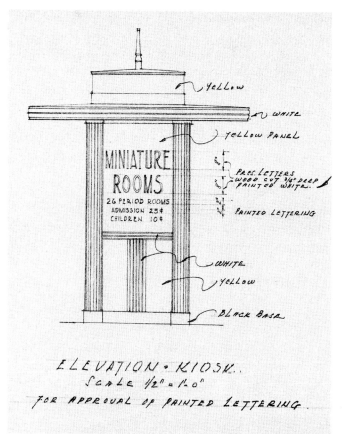

Architect's drawing of the kiosk placed in front of the display of Mrs. Thorne's first set of rooms at the Century of Progress Exposition in Chicago, 1933–34.

an afterthought, perhaps in recognition of the important influence of Oriental design on European decorative styles.) Of the twenty-nine European rooms in the Art Institute, all but one are either English or French. None dates from earlier than the 16th century. There are no ancient or medieval rooms; no rooms from Italy, Spain, Russia, Scandinavia; and few rooms from the houses of any but the well-to-do. There is just one room representing Germany (E-28). (Mrs. Thorne did create another German room—a Rococo hallway—which was initially exhibited with both sets of rooms. It was dismantled around the time that the rooms were placed in their present gallery in the Art Institute.) The rooms are arranged precisely in chronological sequence, with the greatest proportion (13 of 31, or 40 percent) depicting interiors from the 18th century. There are only four rooms from the 19th century and only two from the 20th.

But Mrs. Thorne was not concerned with being comprehensive; that would have been impossible to accomplish. For the most part, she chose to portray the styles and periods she felt were significant. As we have seen, for Mrs. Thorne and others of similar background, the grace of English and French interiors during the 18th century was *the* standard of good taste and breeding. Her notes contain references to her belief that in the 18th century, interior design reached its zenith, and it was this period that provided the styles with which she surrounded herself in her everyday life. Thus, the European Rooms, taken as a whole, can be seen as a reminder of a style of living that had virtually come to an end with World War I.

The second set of rooms was shown along with the first set at the World's Fairs in San Francisco and New York, in 1939 and 1940, respectively. Extensive publicity accompanied the rooms, including major articles in newspapers and in *Life* magazine. In the course of the next few years the rooms traveled to such cities as Baltimore, St. Louis, Boston, and Washington, D.C.

Not one to rest on her laurels, Mrs. Thorne now embarked on a set of 37 American Rooms to complement the European ones. These were designed and executed between 1937 and 1940. As with the European Rooms, Mrs. Thorne's selection of places and periods is revealing. Of the thirty-seven rooms, twenty-one date from the 18th century and all but eight depict interiors on the East Coast.

Certainly, Mrs. Thorne's selections can be accounted for, in part, by the fact that the East Coast was settled first and therefore displayed the greatest variety in interior design. But, her choices seem to have been determined as well by a conviction, held by most experts of her day, that in America the dominant and most important cultures were those of the Atlantic Seaboard, New England, and the Old South. Examples of such styles as Arts and Crafts, Art Nouveau, Prairie School, and Bauhaus modernism are noticeably absent. Only three rooms—from the West and Southwest—are contemporary ones, and the one room representing the entire Midwest (A-33) dates from the post-Civil War era. Once again, as she had with the European Rooms, Mrs. Thorne seems to have chosen periods and styles she admired and with which she was most familiar.

Thus, what we have in the Thorne European and American Rooms is not *the* history of interior design, but *a* history. That history was Mrs. Thorne's; she had her own vision of what was important, and she followed it.

Mrs. Thorne presented all three sets of rooms to The Art Institute of Chicago in 1940. Shortly afterwards, the museum sold the first set of 30 rooms to the IBM Corporation, which, in turn, sent them on tour for a number of years. In 1960 Mrs. Thorne's son Niblack happened to see some of them on display in a New York store window. They were, in his words, "the worse for wear." Years of travel had taken a heavy toll on the fragile rooms. Through the generosity of IBM, Niblack Thorne arranged to have the rooms returned to Mrs. Thorne. Repairs were made and the rooms were extensively refurbished. Sixteen of them were then donated to the Phoenix Art Museum in Phoenix, Arizona, as a tribute to Niblack Thorne's late wife, Marie. Nine of the rooms were presented by IBM to the Dulin Gallery of Art in Knoxville, Tennessee, at about the same time. The remaining rooms were dismantled. Today both the Phoenix Museum and the Dulin Gallery have the rooms on permanent display. The Art Institute's Thorne Rooms were installed permanently in the museum in 1954 with a fund Mrs. Thorne provided for their exhibition and care.

A personal triumph for Mrs. Thorne occurred in 1936, when she escorted members of the British royal family through an exhibition of her second set of rooms. Later, she was told that the family would accept a room made by her, and so she created an interior depicting a library in Windsor Castle. She intended it as a gift for the coronation of Edward VIII. When Edward abdicated, the room entered the collection of the Victoria and Albert Museum, London.

Mrs. Thorne continued to work with miniatures for the remainder of her long life, but she never again produced such rooms for public display. She did, however, make

many more modest rooms for her son Niblack and for friends and relatives in the Chicago area. In her last years she began to make shadow boxes, many of which were sold through the Woman's Exchange for charity. Shortly before her death in 1966 she created two rooms for Children's Memorial Hospital in Chicago.

In her late miniatures Mrs. Thorne broke away from her earlier emphasis on periods to include Parisian street scenes with people and soldiers, and fanciful interiors with Peter Rabbit and other Beatrix Potter characters. She also continued to create dining rooms and parlors. She seems to have loved miniature books, for among her later works are libraries and bookstores with curved windows displaying their wares.

* * *

While complete records on the making of the rooms do not exist, the Art Institute's files do contain Mrs. Thorne's lecture notes on the European rooms, hundreds of sketches and blueprints both for the rooms and the individual items within them, and some references to her research sources. Through these materials, and through interviews with the few people still alive who worked on the rooms or who were close to Mrs. Thorne, it is possible to catch a glimpse of her working methods.

Although many people worked on the Thorne Rooms, all available information indicates that Mrs. Thorne conceived the ideas for each of the rooms, provided many of the antiques that went into them from her large collection, and made all of the final decisions about the furnishings. The hired craftsmen who made much of the furniture, especially for the American Rooms, worked under her direction, as did friends from such organizations as the Needlework and Textile Guild of Chicago, founded in the mid-1930s as a source for custom needlework.

Many names appear in the Art Institute files. Most of them are unidentified, so it is difficult to determine which ones represent hired workmen and which ones friends, except that craftsmen are usually cited by last name only. For example, a man referred to as Brundel did a considerable amount of work for Mrs. Thorne. He was responsible for over 40 pieces of furniture in 13 rooms.

In 1936 Mrs. Thorne was invited by the British royal family to create a miniature replica of a library in Windsor Castle. Completed the following year, it was placed in the Victoria and Albert Museum, London.

The large rug in the Early Georgian Drawing Room (E-7) was designed by Miss Dorothy Douville and executed by Miss Scott. Both were connected with the Needlework and Textile Guild of Chicago. Miss Percell is credited with the upholstery of the red and white chair in the New England Bedroom (A-13).

On the other hand, the contributions and identities of some of the other workers are well known. Francis W. Kramer, a window-display artist for Marshall Field & Company, is credited with building the exterior walls and support shelves into which each room fits for 95 of the rooms Mrs. Thorne completed. A Danish-born craftsman, A. W. Pederson, served as full-time foreman for Mrs. Thorne between 1932 and 1939. He decorated many of the Thorne Rooms, painted china, did finishing work on much of the furniture, and painted most of the outdoor scenes. Another artist, German-born sculptor Alfons Weber, who had also worked on displays at Marshall Field & Company, executed the elaborate ornamental carvings in several of the European Rooms.

The Department of Architecture at The Art Institute of Chicago has in its archives the architectural drawings for most of the Thorne Rooms. Plans and elevations for nine of the European Rooms and one of the American were signed by Edwin H. Clark, a prominent Chicago architect who also designed the library in Mrs. Thorne's apartment on North Lake Shore Drive. The fact that Mrs. Thorne engaged an established architect to execute such detailed drawings shows the seriousness with which she treated the construction of her miniature rooms.

The Thorne Room files contain 569 detailed drawings of furniture, mirrors, sconces, ottomans, footstools, clocks, and chandeliers, each drawn to scale. Nearly all of them are unsigned. From other material we can surmise that a great many of these drawings were executed by Ralph Wheeler, a draftsman who worked for the firm of Watson & Boaler in Chicago. Although none of these is signed, some do carry the name Boaler, Burchell & Dillon Inc., presumably successors of Watson & Boaler.

In all, some three dozen people appear to have participated in the construction of the Thorne Rooms. Perhaps

17

Mrs. Thorne purchased from Arthur Punt, a noted London dealer in antique miniatures, almost every object pictured in this advertisement. The two Queen Anne chairs, for example, are to be found in Room A-5, while the checkerboard table at the right was placed in E-9.

the best way to appreciate how the Thorne Rooms were built is to look at the very different contributions of two individuals.

The first is Arthur Punt, who ran a shop on Francis Street in London. A leading European dealer in miniatures, Punt was one of Mrs. Thorne's favorite sources during her collecting days. Indeed, many of the pieces featured in the advertisement reproduced here were purchased by Mrs. Thorne and were later incorporated into various rooms.

A source that Mrs. Thorne did *not* identify was a "little shop in Paris" where she acquired many of her most precious items. To her dying day she refused to divulge the name or the location of the store, despite repeated entreaties from other miniaturists. Dealers like Punt and the owner of the little shop in Paris were established if not common fixtures in the European antique market, and Mrs. Thorne relied heavily upon them.

The other person who was important in the history of the Thorne Rooms is Eugene Kupjack. When he went to work for Mrs. Thorne in the late 1930s, Kupjack was a young man. He arrived after the European Rooms were finished, but his work appears in every American Room. After Mrs. Thorne's projects were completed, Kupjack went into the business of making miniatures for himself.

Today in his seventies, Kupjack, still a Chicago-area resident, is considered by many to be the dean of American miniaturists.

Kupjack's interviews through the years afford us first-hand accounts of how Mrs. Thorne worked. Mrs. Thorne may have contracted for many services, she may have done only some of the actual handiwork herself, but her vision controlled the entire enterprise. Kupjack has likened her to Walt Disney, a conceptual mastermind whose touch is manifested in every object, in every corner of every room. Mrs. Thorne decided which rooms to depict, she hired the draftsmen and architects to draw up the plans, she made the assignments, and she approved the final products.

Since the rooms were built in large sets, inevitably there was something of the assembly line in Mrs. Thorne's studio. At any one time, several rooms were being worked on at once. Nonetheless, each room was constructed and furnished in a manner best suited to its particular needs. Patience was the order of the day, for the technology of model construction was a good deal less advanced 50 years ago. In our age of wonder glues and plastics, it is easy to forget that Mrs. Thorne's workmen used old-fashioned materials. Animal glue was the principal bonding agent, and it had to be applied when it was hot. Today's casein glues would have made the work far easier. Rubber and plastic molds, common in all forms of interior design work today, were unknown. As a result, much of the decorative ceiling moldings, wainscoting, and the like had to be done by hand, using regular plaster. Epoxies simply did not exist.

Perhaps the greatest tribute to Mrs. Thorne's team of craftsmen is the way in which the hundreds of objects that they created in a few short years blend so perfectly with laboriously detailed antiques. The workmanship on the antiques is often extraordinary: the clock in the Massachusetts Drawing Room (A-5) can actually run; the tiny locks in the furniture drawers of two pieces in the Louis XVI Salon (E-24) actually turn; the rug in the Late Jacobean Drawing Room (E-4) is a genuine, hand-woven antique. Side by side with such marvelous gems are improvised creations. The tray of the copper tea set in the Cape Cod Living Room (A-12) is fashioned from an American copper penny. The bases of the tureens on the table and sideboard in Virginia Dining Room—Gunston Hall (A-20) are made from silver Liberty dimes, while the wine coolers on the side table are fashioned out of French 20-centime pieces dated 1867. Some of the "porcelains" in the Thorne Rooms are genuine antiques, some were carved from ivory, and still others were hand-carved in wood which was then coated with layer after layer of casein until the surface acquired the appropriate luminosity. Petit-point evening bags were called into service as rugs, while upholstery and scarves were converted into draperies. Just as the scenic designer in the theater uses little tricks to fool the eye of the audience, so Mrs. Thorne and her team performed whatever magic they could to create the perfect illusion.

Mrs. Thorne seems to have found her craftsmen through good luck and persistence. The Depression had thrown many skilled people out of work, and Mrs. Thorne was in a position to hire the finest talents available in a way that a more prosperous era might not have allowed. Edwin H. Clark, the architect who did many of the plans and elevations for the Thorne Rooms, was the designer of such important Chicago landmarks as the Lincoln Park Administration Building, Winnetka Village Hall, and Brookfield Zoo. It is hardly likely that a man of such distinction would have been available to design miniature rooms had it not been for the building slump brought about by the Depression.

* * *

Architects in real life face numerous constraints which force choices on them: the size of the land plot, the number of rooms needed by the client, the money available, the materials to be used, the function of the building, and so forth. Mrs. Thorne faced no such limitations; she could depict any type, size, or shape of room she wanted. How did she decide which colors, materials, ground plans, and decorative features to use? The task was enormous, but Mrs. Thorne attacked it with zeal and determination.

She had first to pick which rooms to create in miniature. As we have seen, she clearly had in mind what periods were important and should therefore be represented. In some instances, she knew of a room that was close enough to her conception to warrant copying. In other cases, she was forced to invent a "typical" room because she did not have access to a suitable model.

When she chose to depict an extant room, how did she determine what it looked like in a previous era? All stately homes undergo transformations through the years: one owner adds a wall, another tears it down; one owner loves wainscoting, another dislikes it. A room that Mrs. Thorne may have actually seen in the 1930s is likely to have looked entirely different when it was first built. Paintings, drawings, sketches, diaries, and letters may indicate the nature of those changes, but an absolute reconstruction is an impossibility.

The problem is aggravated even further in the case of furnishings. Fashions and tastes alter remarkably rapidly, and people change their furnishings even faster than they replace walls or wainscoting. Rare is the house, royal or otherwise, that does not freely mix periods and styles of furniture and appointments. Mrs. Thorne had to guess how each of her rooms might have been furnished during the period in which she chose to depict it.

Mrs. Thorne's problems were no less complex in working with the "typical" rooms. It is possible to determine through countless measurements of countless rooms what the "typical" proportions of architecture in any given period were. But no room is "typical" any more than any single human being is "typical." Thus, she had to take ideas and details from various sources and combine them in such a way that they appear convincing as a whole.

Another problem she faced was one posed by the physical nature of miniature rooms and dollhouses. Because the Thorne Rooms all have one wall "missing" to enable us to look into them, they are, in effect, miniature stage sets.

Mrs. Thorne took a cue from the conventions of stage design as she went about the task of laying out her rooms. According to those conventions, furniture, wall features, doors, and windows must be arranged somewhat artificially to ensure that nothing blocks the "audience's" point of view. Basically, everything that would normally go on or against four walls must be placed against three. Mrs. Thorne had the unenviable task, therefore, of changing

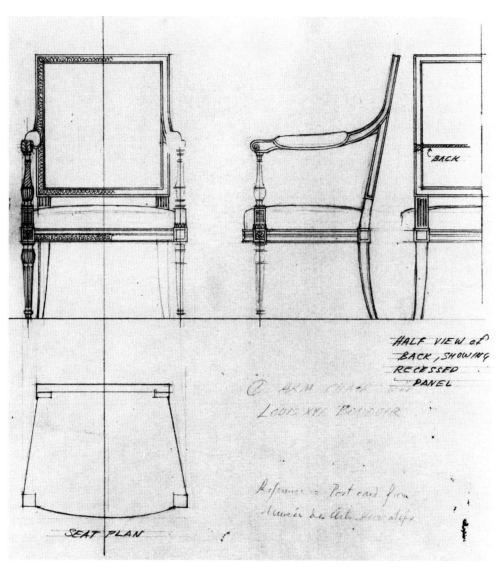

Mrs. Thorne often used postcards depicting objects from museum collections as models for the furniture in her interiors. The postcard to the left, illustrating a Louis XVI armchair from the Musée des Arts Décoratifs, Paris, was translated into the working drawing for the French Salon (E-24), to the right.

historic details without appearing to change them, a task that she managed with great flair.

One way to appreciate both the conceptual and practical problems involved in creating the miniature rooms is to examine the drawings for both the rooms and the furnishings within them. We have chosen to focus on two of the rooms, one European and one American. This will enable us to understand the kinds of questions Mrs. Thorne had to answer before the first piece of wood was cut, the first paint jar opened.

Room E-24 is described as a Salon of the period of Louis XVI. Mrs. Thorne dated the room at about 1780. Many fine examples of such rooms still stand in such buildings as the Petit Trianon and the palace at Versailles and the château of Fontainebleau. With so many models to choose from, why did Mrs. Thorne invent her own version? The answer lies in the furnishings.

We know from notes and files that the writing desk on the right wall and the small chest on the wall next to the fireplace are pieces that Mrs. Thorne had in her collection. She bought them from the anonymous little antique shop in Paris. Because she owned such fine pieces, it is likely that she decided to build a room around them. It is probably no accident that these two objects occupy such prominent positions in the room.

Once she decided to use these pieces, the rest of the floor plan must have fallen easily into place. Any salon from this period would have had a fireplace, at least two entrance doors, and French windows. Mrs. Thorne's visits to French buildings of the period would have told her as much. The floor plan of the room shows that these obligatory elements, added to the two antique pieces, account for most of the available space.

Only a settee and a few side pieces were needed to complete the room. These Mrs. Thorne commissioned. The drawings for most of these objects—the settee, armchair, two side chairs, end table, small table, book stands, and mirror frame—are in the Art Institute's files. All of the drawings have the sources written right on them, so we know what the models were for every piece in the room. The settee, armchair, and lyre-back chair were all taken from postcards from the Musée des Arts Décoratifs in Paris. These postcards have been preserved; one is reproduced here next to the drawing made from it. The other pieces were all taken from Mrs. Thorne's reference books, one being G. Henriot's *Les Beaux Meubles des collections privées,* and the other, S. de Ricci's *Louis XVI Furniture.* These volumes and a handful of others—which are cited time and again on the drawings—are large picture books, each containing hundreds of photographic plates. They are a small portion of an extensive library of reference books on decorative arts, architecture, and interiors that Mrs. Thorne assembled and consulted.

A different situation exists for the Virginia Dining Room (A-22), inspired by Kenmore, a house in Fredericksburg, Virginia, which still stands today. A detailed comparison between Mrs. Thorne's miniature and the actual dining room at Kenmore reveals several important differences. The first is the fact that the two doors on the rear wall which are set flush to the corners at the real Kenmore have been moved slightly toward the center of the room in the miniature (see pages 22–23). The effect of liberating the doors from the corners is a spaciousness not present in the original.

The next two variations are more substantial. The rear wall in Mrs. Thorne's version is plastered, whereas the original is paneled. Mrs. Thorne's room also contains an elaborate plastered overmantel which never existed in the dining room at Kenmore. There are, however, similar decorative overmantels in the drawing room and the library at Kenmore; indeed, the plasterwork is considered one of the outstanding features of the house. We know that it was done by an anonymous Frenchman some 20 years after the house was built in 1752 (the year that Mrs. Thorne gives for her reproduction). Mrs. Thorne transposed the overmantel from the library into the dining room, clearly believing that it was too fine a feature to leave out. Once again, her desire to depict the general feeling of Kenmore outweighed demands for literal fidelity.

The most interesting feature of this room is the use of window-doors on the left wall. Present-day Kenmore has built-in window seats where Mrs. Thorne placed her

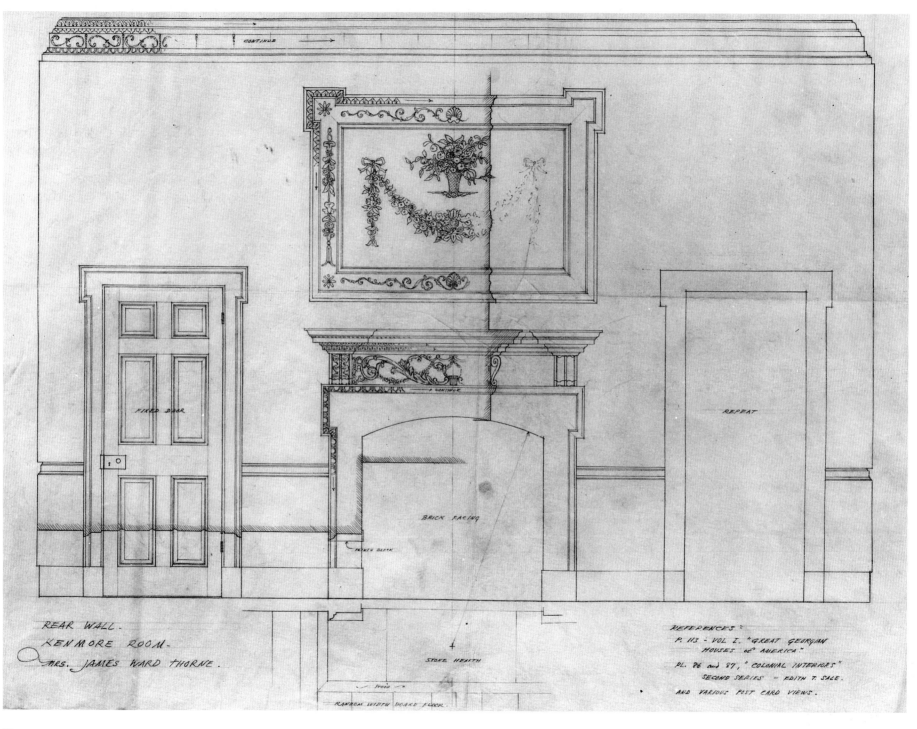

CONTINUE →

FIXED DOOR

REPEAT

BRICK FACING

FRENCH BLOCK

REAR WALL.

KENMORE ROOM.

MRS. JAMES WARD THORNE.

STONE HEARTH

WOOD

RANDOM WIDTH BOARD FLOOR.

REFERENCES:

P. 113 - VOL I. "GREAT GEORGIAN
HOUSES OF AMERICA"

PL. 86 and 87, "COLONIAL INTERIORS"
SECOND SERIES - EDITH T. SALE.

AND VARIOUS POST CARD VIEWS.

window-doors. Such window-doors are not a feature typical of 18th-century Virginia homes. Mrs. Thorne copied the design, as the architect's elevation clearly notes, from Ricciuti's book *New Orleans and Its Environs*. We also know that the window seat which is in front of the rear window-door in the miniature was designed after an illustration in *American Antique Furniture* by E. Miller, Jr.

A comparison between the architect's drawing of Mrs. Thorne's interior of the Virginia Dining Room at Kenmore (A-22), on the left, and a photograph of the actual room, above, shows some of the adjustments made by Mrs. Thorne. These included moving the doors toward the center and replacing the paneled overmantle with a replica of the elaborate plasterwork from another room in the house.

Working drawing of the mirror on the window wall in Mrs. Thorne's representation of the dining room at Kenmore, derived from a figure in Wallace Nutting's Furniture Treasury, *a reference book Mrs. Thorne consulted frequently.*

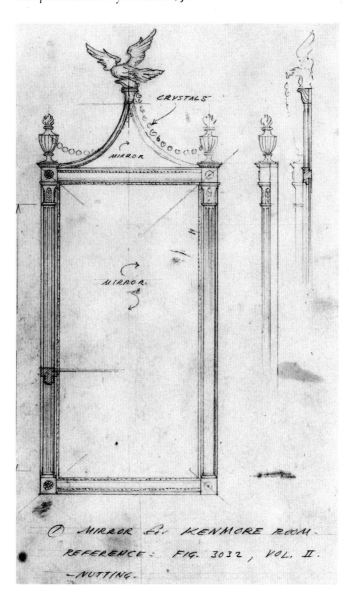

CRYSTALS

MIRROR

MIRROR

① MIRROR for KENMORE ROOM.
REFERENCE: FIG. 3032, VOL. II.
— NUTTING.

Why did she go to such great lengths to change the room? In an interview Eugene Kupjack offered a likely explanation. Mrs. Thorne had an overwhelming passion for symmetry. She wished all of her rooms to be shown head-on. She also demanded that they be perfectly balanced. It could well be that Mrs. Thorne saw in the evolving design for Kenmore that there was a risk of serious imbalance. The two heavy commodes and the heavy wooden door on the right wall were in danger of overpowering the light, airy window wall. She may have thought that the best way to preserve symmetry was to add the window-doors and to place furniture in front of them.

The sources for the furniture and furnishings are well documented. The twin commodes, sideboard, and mirror were taken from Wallace Nutting's *Furniture Treasury*. The window seat and the drop-leaf table in the anteroom were copied from illustrations in *American Antique Furniture* by E. Miller, Jr. L. V. Lockwood's *Colonial Furniture in America* was the source for the dining-room table. The side chairs, armchairs, and chandelier were all inspired by magazine clippings and a postcard which have since been lost. Mr. Kupjack recalls building all of the furniture except for the commodes. These were done by Mr. Brundel. The silver pieces were executed by John C. Moore of Tiffany's workshop in New York, whose hallmark appears on them. They are genuine antiques. Also interesting are the hurricane lamps. Mr. Kupjack engraved the eagles on the lucite chimneys according to Mrs. Thorne's directions.

In the late 1970s a visitor to the Thorne Rooms noticed the eagles and wrote to the Art Institute, asking how Fielding Lewis, the builder of Kenmore who died in 1781, could have owned lamps bearing the national symbol which was not adopted until 1782. The Art Institute has decided not to change or correct any inaccuracies, anachronisms, or anomalies in the Thorne Rooms. The rooms are Mrs. Thorne's creation, and to alter anything within them would violate her work. In the final analysis, it is the unity of her vision that should prevail in her rooms.

The Thorne Rooms are approaching the half-century mark in age, and the wear caused by road shows, constant exhibition, and simple deterioration is a source of natural concern. One particular problem has been the tremendous amount of heat generated by the incandescent bulbs that illuminate the rooms; the Art Institute, as of this writing, is installing new lighting. Through the years, chairs have come unglued, wallpaper has peeled, colors have faded, just as they would in real life. The draperies in the Empire Anteroom (E-26), for example, had faded from a brilliant green to a pale gold. An emerald-green cloth which matched the chairs was finally procured to replace the old curtains. Similarly, the floral arrangements on the furniture and the foliage in the gardens need constant care. Replacements that match the originals as closely as possible are ordered whenever needed. Today, Alice Pirie Hargrave, Technical Assistant for the Thorne Rooms since 1977, and a team of loyal volunteers tend to the rooms, dusting with a camel's-hair brush, changing burned-out bulbs, replacing objects that have become dislodged, and checking for serious wear. Windows and chandeliers are washed regularly, and the furniture is polished and re-upholstered as needed. The silver, copper, and brass are all polished at regular intervals. With 68 rooms, each filled with scores of irreplaceable objects, maintenance is an endless and meticulous task. The efforts of Mrs. Thorne and her craftsmen certainly deserve no less.

* * *

In the final analysis, the Thorne Miniature Rooms provide an intense experience of a most particular kind. We noted earlier how Mrs. Thorne used the conventions of the stage in laying out her floor plans. Many people, including Mrs. Thorne, have described the rooms as being theatrical, as being like tiny stage sets just waiting for the actors to make their appearances.

The Thorne Rooms are indeed a form of theater. The glass through which we see the rooms is the exact equivalent of the curtain in a proscenium theater: it shapes and limits our view. We cannot stand inside any of the Thorne Rooms any more than we can stand on a stage while a play is in progress. Our viewpoint is a single one, the one which the set designer (in this case, Mrs. Thorne) allows us to see. We can move our heads from one corner of the glass to another, we can crane our necks to view what is outside

of the tiny windows in each room, but ultimately we are limited to just one point of view.

Whereas in a full-sized period room, we can walk about (unless there are ropes keeping us on narrow carpets) and look at the objects and space from several points of view, in the Thorne Rooms Mrs. Thorne, the master illusionist, is completely in charge of what we see. We trust that illusionist, we put our faith in her ability to charm us, and we enjoy the tricks she uses to entertain. In the theater this phenomenon is called "the willing suspension of disbelief." It is no different with the Thorne Rooms. We know the rooms are not real, we know that we are being fooled, and we adore the experience.

But the essential theatricality of the Thorne Rooms lies deeper still. It has to do with the absence of any human figures. Mrs. Thorne did use figures in both earlier and later rooms, with varying degrees of success. Eugene Kupjack, when asked why Mrs. Thorne did not use human figures in the Art Institute rooms, suggested that she abandoned their use because she had such difficulty making them appear realistic enough. In her notes Mrs. Thorne discussed her preference for using little objects—balls of yarn, tea cups, opened books—to suggest the presence of human beings.

It is the very absence of figures which makes the Art Institute Thorne Rooms so compelling. Their creator did not supply them, so we, the audience, must. The rooms are somehow incomplete until we exercise our imagination and populate this amazing miniature world. As we stand in the darkened galleries, our faces pressed against the glass, alone or perhaps with one other person, we enter a private world. We wonder what it would be like to live in such a room, what grand and splendid people might be there with us—and we do this through a tiny window frame. We must furnish the crucial missing ingredient—life—which is why we can stand riveted in front of our favorite rooms for so long. We are not just the audience any more, we are the playwright and the stage director as well. The Thorne Rooms become for us a springboard into our own imaginations, a vast array of stage sets waiting for the drama that only our fantasies can create.

*Each year thousands of visitors view
the Thorne Miniature Rooms displayed in
connecting galleries at The Art Institute
of Chicago.*

EUROPEAN ROOMS

1. English Great Hall of the Late Tudor Period, 1550–1603
2. English Bedchamber of the Jacobean or Stuart Period, 1603–88
3. English Reception Room of the Jacobean Period, 1625–55
4. English Drawing Room of the Late Jacobean Period, 1680–1702
5. English Cottage Kitchen of the Queen Anne Period, 1702–14
6. English Library of the Queen Anne Period, 1702–50
7. English Drawing Room of the Early Georgian Period, 1730s
8. English Bedroom of the Georgian Period, 1760–75
9. English Drawing Room of the Georgian Period, 1770–1800
10. English Dining Room of the Georgian Period, 1770–90
11. English Entrance Hall of the Georgian Period, c. 1775
12. English Drawing Room of the Georgian Period, c. 1800
13. English Rotunda and Library of the Regency Period, 1810–20
14. English Drawing Room of the Victorian Period, 1840–70
15. English Drawing Room of the Modern Period, 1930s
16. French Hall of the Louis XII Period, c. 1500
17. French Bedroom, Late 16th Century
18. French Salon of the Louis XIV Period, 1660–1700
19. French Dining Room of the Louis XIV Period, 1660–1700
20. French Library of the Louis XV Period, c. 1720
21. French Boudoir of the Louis XV Period, 1740–60
22. French Provincial Bedroom of the Louis XV Period, 18th Century
23. French Dining Room of the Periods of Louis XV and Louis XVI, 1760–80
24. French Salon of the Louis XVI Period, c. 1780
25. French Bathroom and Boudoir of the Revolutionary Period, 1793–1804
26. French Anteroom of the Empire Period, c. 1810
27. French Library of the Modern Period, 1930s
28. German Sitting Room of the "Biedermeier" Period, 1815–50
29. English Roman Catholic Church in the Gothic Style, Late 13th Century
30. Chinese Interior, Traditional
31. Japanese Interior, Traditional

These items, drawn from the European miniature rooms made by Mrs. James Ward Thorne and now in The Art Institute of Chicago, are pictured in their actual sizes based on a scale of one inch to a foot. The armchair is from Room E-11; the tea table from E-21; the cabinet from E-4; the harpsichord, stool, flowers, and tea set from E-12; and the rug from E-28.

In the measurements listed for each room, height precedes width precedes depth. Measurements reflect those of main rooms only; side and back rooms are not included. In rooms with curved ceilings height has been measured to the top of the cornice.

1. English Great Hall of the Late Tudor Period, 1550–1603

What intrigued Mrs. Thorne about the late Tudor period was the transformation of Britain's feudal castles from "armed strongholds" into "homelike dwellings built for pleasure and comfort," as she put it. She regarded the "furnishing of the bare and cheerless rooms of these castles [as being] in the nature of a new experiment," and applauded the English nobility for seeking guidance from Italy, whose artisans had been creating fine tapestries, brocades, and elaborately carved furniture for more than a century. Italian Renaissance motifs and styles also reached England by way of the Netherlands, modified by Dutch craftsmen.

A number of these influences are apparent in this hall, a composite of several admired by Mrs. Thorne. The elaborate ceiling, walls, chimney piece, refectory table, wainscot (paneled) chair, and floor were modeled after examples in Parham Park, Sussex, built in 1577. A recent history of that house points out, however, that while the Tudor paneling has always been in the house, the floor is probably from the 18th century.

The massive carved screen, topped by elaborate strapwork concealing a minstrel gallery, is copied from Wadham College, Oxford, built between 1610 and 1613. Strapwork (so called because of its resemblance to interwoven leather straps) was very popular in the Netherlands; it incorporates grotesque motifs of classical origin revived by Italian Renaissance artists. A similar screen and gallery are to be found in the hall of Knole Castle, Kent, installed during Elizabeth I's reign by Thomas, first Earl of Dorset, who employed a private orchestra to play for him while he dined.

The furniture chosen by Mrs. Thorne illustrates the types of forms available at the time, though inventories from houses of that period suggest that fewer types and fewer pieces would have been used in any single room. The Tudor settle to the left of the fireplace shows how the traditional dower chest (bearing a bride's dowry) evolved into a seating facility through the addition of a panel back and arms. The carving on the settle and the cupboard (to the right of the fireplace) displays an Italian influence. The base of the slope-top desk by the window bay is modeled on a 16th-century piece described in one of Mrs. Thorne's sources as "one of the earliest individual English desks . . . probably made in a monastery to be used as a lectern."

The portrait above the settle is of Christina, Duchess of Milan (offered as a bride to Henry VIII), after a portrait by Hans Holbein the Younger; the one above the cupboard depicts Mary, Queen of Scots. Over the fireplace is a copy of Pisanello's *Vision of St. Eustache* in the National Gallery, London. Above the chair on the extreme right is a portrait of Henry VIII.

Although the armor is of the period of Henry VIII, it is not likely to have been displayed in this fashion. In its total effect, however, the room clearly conveys Mrs. Thorne's intention. The hall of medieval times—the communal living room of rough and ready warriors—has been transformed into a place of comfort, cheer, and some splendor.

This room measures 23 × 25¼ × 31¾ inches.

2. English Bedchamber of the Jacobean or Stuart Period, 1603–88

The 85 years between the accession to the throne of the first Stuart king, James I, in 1603 and the expulsion of James II in 1688, encompassed the beheading of Charles I, 11 years of the Puritan Commonwealth under the dictatorship of Oliver Cromwell, the exuberant period of the Restoration under Charles II (brought back from exile in France), and the Glorious Revolution in which James II was deposed and William of Orange and Mary (a Stuart) were brought to the throne. The term Jacobean, which is given to this period, comes from Jacobus, the Latin origin of the name James.

Mrs. Thorne was impressed by the fine Jacobean rooms at Knole Castle, Kent, which was presented to Thomas Sackville by his cousin Elizabeth I. Architecturally, this bedchamber reproduces rather faithfully the paneled walls, window recess, and mantel from what is known as the Spangled Bedroom at Knole. The taste for ornate, carved decoration—inherited from the Elizabethan period—is seen in the fireplace, window embrasures, and furniture.

The press cupboard to the left of the fireplace and the chest to the right of the bed are early Jacobean, but much of the remaining furniture is of a later date. For example, the high-canopied bed, draped in damask, is in the style introduced to England by Charles II and his court, and reflects the influence of their exile in France, where the nobility received callers while abed. The original bed in the Knole bedchamber, which inspired this interior, sported curtains with appliqué strapwork decorated with metallic spangles, from which that room derived its name.

The dressing table in front of the window is also of the later Jacobean period; its fittings, too, bear a close resemblance to those at Knole. After the mid-17th century, walnut became the most fashionable wood for furniture. The daybed is modeled after a walnut original from about 1670, and the high-back chair between the bed and the chest after a model of 1688.

The needlepoint picture above the prie-dieu to the right of the fireplace and the tapestry above the cupboard were made in Vienna; the silver pieces and candlestick on the dressing table and on the stands, as well as the bowl and ewer on the table to the left of the bed, were made in England.

The flowers and the view through the window reflect Mrs. Thorne's de-

light in the gardens at Knole. "Some friends have asked me why I put flowers in my early English rooms— they rather doubted this delicate touch," she wrote, "so I was particularly pleased to see in a book on *Life in Elizabethan Days* this sentence, 'The coming of the Renaissance accentuated all the natural human love of flowers and greenery.'" She had heard, as well, that Elizabeth I had planted a rose bush outside the Spangled Bedroom at Knole, and through the centuries the gardeners had continued to cultivate Queen Elizabeth roses.

This room measures 17 × 27½ × 24¼ inches.

3. English Reception Room of the Jacobean Period, 1625–55

When I visited Wilton, I was deeply impressed by the magnificence of these royal apartments," wrote Mrs. Thorne, describing portions of the magnificent house designed for Philip, fourth Earl of Pembroke, by architect Inigo Jones. The earl, Lord Chamberlain to King Charles I, turned to Jones on the king's recommendation after his house had burned in a fire. Jones brought to the design of Wilton the Italian influences he had absorbed as a student in that country. A disciple of Andrea Palladio's classicism, Jones was also much impressed by the rich ornament of the Italian Baroque.

These influences are easily discerned in this interior. Here, Mrs. Thorne drew on two lavish rooms at Wilton—the so-called Single Cube Room (which measures 30×30×30 feet) and the so-called Double Cube Room (60×60×60 feet). Both rooms feature painted white paneling that is richly carved from floor (dado) to ceiling (cornice). In her interior Mrs. Thorne substituted red damask for the paneling, confining the gilded carving to the ceiling, cornice, overmantel, and door and window frames. The elaborate painted ceiling, mirrors, and gilded furniture—distinctly Italianate in inspiration—convey the spirit of opulence that pervades the state reception rooms at Wilton.

The overmantel, ceiling center, and door are modeled after those of the Single Cube Room but are less elaborate. The floor is copied from another Inigo Jones commission, the Queen's House in Greenwich. The tables resemble originals by William Kent, a follower of Inigo Jones, who had also studied in Italy and who favored solid side tables on thick scrolled supports decorated with classical masks, swags, and leaf ornaments.

The copies of the van Dyck portraits refer to the numerous family portraits executed by that artist for the owners of Wilton in the 1630s. Provision for displaying the portraits was made in the design of the Double Cube and of other state rooms.

The window looks out onto a narrow walled walk fronting a garden with a lake.

This room measures 16¼ × 24½ × 19¼ inches.

4. English Drawing Room of the Late Jacobean Period, 1680–1702

In 1685 William Winde designed Belton House for the Bronlow family of Lincolnshire. A very fine residence, it was conceived in the manner of Sir Christopher Wren, architect of St. Paul's Cathedral, London, and the single most influential figure in English architecture in the decades after the Great Fire of London of 1666. Mrs. Thorne was particularly drawn to the library, with its "elaborate carving over the mantel and between the panels . . . attributed to Grinling Gibbons—a woodcarver of great ability." She also admired the ceilings throughout the house, with their dramatic high-relief moldings of fruits and flowers. These influences are evident in this interior.

By the time that Belton House was completed in 1689, the Glorious Revolution had brought to the throne James II's Protestant daughter, Mary, and her Dutch husband, Prince William of Orange. With them came a wave of new fashions in household appointments. The cabinet against the left wall, copied from a piece featuring oyster, ivory, and wood inlays, exhibits the complex marquetry patterns that were inspired by French and Dutch examples. Tall case clocks like the one shown here became popular at this time. The stool, tall-back chairs, cabinet, and table by the fireplace are from the same period. The pair of black side

tables are "japanned" to imitate Oriental lacquer. The secretary against the right wall, the cabinet, and the clock came from the London shop of Arthur Punt.

An excellent needlewoman, Queen Mary created a vogue for needlepoint-covered chairs and settees like the ones in this room. The rug was found in an antique shop in Paris. Soiled beyond recognition, it turned out to be a miniature of a Near Eastern carpet when cleaned. During the 17th century, such rugs tended to be used as table rather than floor coverings.

Dutch Delftware (tin-glazed earthenware) became highly popular in the mid-17th century. The blue and white coloration had been inspired by Chinese blue and white porcelain imported into the Netherlands by the Dutch East India Company beginning in the early 1600s. The English East India Company imported Oriental ware into England during the 17th century. Mrs. Thorne included both reproductions of Dutch Delft (on the mantel and secretary) and Oriental jade and porcelains (on the cabinet and lacquer tables). The portrait over the mantel is a replica of Anthony van Dyck's 1635 portrait of *Charles I in Hunting Dress,* now in the Musée du Louvre, Paris.

This room measures 16¾ × 26½ × 21⅝ inches.

5. English Cottage Kitchen of the Queen Anne Period, 1702–14

In spite of its designation as a Queen Anne-period room, Mrs. Thorne admitted "that the kitchen which I have reproduced is in the character of Anne Hathaway's cottage [in Stratford-on-Avon]. It has timbered and plastered walls—a large open grate for cooking, and its mullioned windows look out upon an English garden in full bloom. I have visited [this] home many times, and to me it is one of the most appealing shrines of England." She had also visited the Cotswold weavers' cottages made over into weekend retreats by well-to-do Londoners of her own time who had, in her words, "gone bucolic." Like them, she took an eclectic approach to decorating, for although it was inspired by an Elizabethan model, this interior is furnished with pieces from later periods.

The linen fold-paneled settle by the fireplace and the stool (used as a table) beside it were inspired by 17th-century

examples, while the Queen Anne dresser copies an 18th-century type. For the most part, such pieces would have been built of oak, although walnut, elm, and fruitwoods were also used for country furniture. Hoop-and-spindle-back Windsor chairs like the ones included here were popular throughout the 18th century, with yew, a wood that lent itself to being bent, being used to make the hoops.

Many of the menial household tasks in a house of this sort would have been carried out in the scullery, so that the kitchen essentially served as a living room and was furnished accordingly. The wooden ware for daily use would have been kept in the scullery, while the dresser in the kitchen would have contained family treasures—pewter, china, and Staffordshire figures (Staffordshire was actually not prevalent until the late 18th century). The mantel shelf would have served the same purpose, displaying shiny cooking utensils and implements as well.

The flagstone floor indicates that the cottage would have been built directly on the ground with no cellar. During medieval times loose rushes and straw were strewn over the stone floors in both fashionable and ordinary households. The woven rush mattings used subsequently were out of fashion by the mid-17th century. Single widths of various materials served as runners.

The hooked rugs included by Mrs. Thorne in this cottage are out of place: hooked rugs were an American invention popular during the 18th and 19th centuries.

The window looks out onto a flower-filled garden and the thatched roofs of neighboring cottages.

This room measures 10 × 19½ × 16¼ inches.

6. English Library of the Queen Anne Period, 1702–50

Mrs. Thorne's appreciation of English 18th-century decorative arts encompassed a variety of styles. An admirer of the exuberant interiors created by architect Inigo Jones and the elaborate carvings attributed to Grinling Gibbons, she also took pleasure in the simpler lines of what is known as the Queen Anne style, which outlasted by several decades that monarch's 12-year reign (1702–14).

Describing this interior, Mrs. Thorne wrote, "From a manor house in Derbyshire, I have copied a room which suggests the quiet study of an English squire—the ceiling is low, the plain [panels] are painted leaf green, which creates such a flattering background for the rich tones of the walnut furniture."

The style of the furniture in this room belongs, for the most part, to the early Georgian period, or the first quarter of the 18th century. Typical are the side chairs and settee—inspired by Chinese forms—with their curvaceous shapes, vase-like splats, and cabriole legs (curved outward at the knee and tapering into a pad or claw). The Chinese influence is also evident in the black lacquered desk and red lacquered corner cabinet of a somewhat later period modeled after a mid-century example in black and gold. In the 18th century pine or other soft wood was

used for furniture finished in this way. The Oriental note is continued in the porcelain urns on the top shelves of the niches and the carnelian pieces on the chests, tables, and desk.

The two walnut chests, the barometer to the left of the fireplace, and the two miniature globes on the desk were all made in England. The landscape over the fireplace was the top of an old English cardcase; the portrait on the left wall is a rare miniature in oil on panel depicting Lucy, Countess of Sussex. Indirect lighting was common in secondary rooms of this kind and was provided by candles placed on stands—like the tripod by the leather wing chair—and in sconces like the ones flanking the mantel. The books in the two library niches were all individually bound and tooled in England. Mrs. Thorne had a great fondness for miniature books and used them in many of her interiors.

This room measures 13 × 21 × 21⅛ inches.

7. English Drawing Room of the Early Georgian Period, 1730s

This interior was inspired, in part, by a room that had been removed from a London residence, No. 26 Hatton Gardens, and installed in the Victoria and Albert Museum, London. Although the original was done entirely by James Gibbs, Mrs. Thorne also incorporated elements from the work of William Kent—especially in the mantel. Both Gibbs and Kent helped restore in England the popularity of the Palladian and Italian Baroque influences that had characterized the work of Inigo Jones. The advocates of the Palladian revival were patrons and artists who had benefited from the Grand Tour, which by the early 18th century had become a part of the education of the English upper class. The impact of the Palladian revival can be seen in this room in the heavy pedimentation above the fireplace overmantel, doors, and bookcases; and in the marble-topped consoles with their carved eagle supports. These tables and the richly framed mirrors hanging above them were copied from examples executed by Kent.

Typical, too, of this style is the use of niches, here filled with a variety of objects, including ivory painted to resemble porcelain and jade imported from China. On the mantel a carnelian carving is flanked by jade vases. The Oriental theme is carried out in the coromandel lacquer screen, "made by one of the cleverest craftsmen in . . . China by the same process as the old screens." The miniature red and white ivory chessmen set out on the table to the right of the desk, however, were made "by a very big Englishman with proportionately large hands." The silver tea service on the table by the wing chair also was commissioned expressly for this setting.

The rug was presented to Mrs. Thorne by members of the Textile and Needlework Guild of Chicago, the design having been reduced from a Georgian pattern. She referred to it as one of her most cherished possessions. A guild member also executed the needlework upholstery on the chairs flanking the doorway and the desk chair. By the window at the back right stands a functioning architect's table, which here serves as an easel. A small print has been placed on top of it to give the appearance of a painting in progress. The paint brushes are colored needles touched with thick white paint. Thomas Gainsborough's portrait of Mrs. "Perdita" Robinson over the mantel is in the Wallace Collection, London. The view from the window is meant to be Old Regent Street.

This room measures 20 × 31¼ × 24¼ inches.

In 1754 Thomas Chippendale published the first extensive book of currently fashionable furniture designs, *The Gentleman & Cabinet Maker's Director*. This publication and later editions made him so famous that his name was given to many mid-18th-century English furniture styles. Admiring his entrepreneurial spirit, Mrs. Thorne noted, "Up to this time, the work of the cabinetmaker as an individual craftsman had received little recognition beyond a limited circle of customers, but Chippendale knew the art of advertising and his shop at No. 60 St. Martin's Lane was a rendezvous for his fashionable clientele. All the chitchat and gossip of court was retailed amidst the engaging surroundings of beautiful furniture." The *Director* included a wide range of elegant domestic furniture in a variety of styles of the Rococo period (see E-20).

Chippendale's book included designs with an Oriental flavor which came to be known as Chinese Chippendale. An example in this room is the chair to the left of the bed, with its straight, square legs and fretwork. The gold mirror on the right wall and the candle brackets on the left are also copied from designs in Chippendale's book. The source of the striking Chippendale bed, with its pagoda-style, carved canopy, was P. Macquoid's *Dictionary of English Furniture*. The room—especially the wallpaper, candlestand, and sconces—was inspired by an original in Wotton-under-Edge, Gloucestershire, installed in the Victoria and Albert Museum, London. The Chinese had begun to export painted wallpapers to the West in the mid-17th century. They depicted scenes from daily life or flowering trees and birds with colorful plumage, like the paper in this interior.

The widespread interest in Oriental art and motifs reflected in the appointments of this room and others (see E-6) stems from intensive trading with the Orient by many northern European countries. Mrs. Thorne gave much credit for the "Chinese craze" of this period to Sir William Chambers, architect and author of *Designs for Chinese Buildings,* published in 1757. The book had been inspired by several trips Chambers made to the Orient as an employee of the Swedish East India Company. Chambers, who received many important commissions, collaborated with Chippendale on the design of furniture.

The elegant stucco work of the overmantel, with its curving, Rococo scrollwork, demonstrates a favorite 18th-century method of incorporating Blanc-de-chine or polychrome Chinese porcelains into the decor. The fender, grate, and fire irons—all copied from designs of the period—incorporate Chinese fret designs. The torchères in the window bays would have functioned as candlestands. The commode in the left corner has ivory fittings, including a ewer and basin and covered urns. The candlesticks and dressing table accessories were, according to Mrs. Thorne, "the tiniest silver pieces obtainable in London."

This room measures 12 × 19 × 19¼ inches.

9. English Drawing Room of the Georgian Period, 1770–1800

Mrs. Thorne thought of this as her "Hepplewhite" room, commenting, "I have chosen a very simple, late Georgian room, painted white, to be the background for Hepplewhite's diversified types of furniture." George Hepplewhite, an English cabinetmaker, owes much of his reputation to his trade catalogue *The Cabinet-maker and Upholsterer's Guide,* published by his widow in 1788. This book depicts various types of furniture in the styles current during the latter years of Hepplewhite's life, some modified by him to render construction of the pieces less complex. Some of Hepplewhite's finest designs are in the style of the Adam brothers, particularly Robert (see E-10), whose Neoclassical interior decorations and furnishings were highly fashionable in England in the 1760s and '70s, and later in France and in America as well.

The efficient simplicity of the pieces displayed in this room made them particularly satisfying and appealing to Mrs. Thorne. She was pleased by "the grace of line and beauty of contour" of Hepplewhite's designs, noting, however, that he "often followed the extravagances of French designers and in many of his pieces there is a suggestion of Louis XV and Louis XVI in chairs, settees, and consoles." These French influences can be seen in this interior in the lacquered commodes flanking the fireplace and in the oval-back armchairs upholstered in blue. The shield-back chairs, drum-top table, drop-leaf sofa table, and secretary date from the last decade of the 18th century. (The casters on the settee actually rotate.) The commodes were copied from ones made around 1770 for the Marquess of Salisbury's Hatfield House. Hepplewhite recommended the use of satinwood, which he often inlaid with other exotic woods.

On the floor is a reproduction of an English version of a rug in the style made originally in the French carpet factories at Aubusson. The fireplace overmantel was inspired by an original (c. 1730) from Marlow Place, in Buckinghamshire, illustrated in M. Jourdain's *English Interiors in Smaller Houses.* Finely tooled leather-covered books fill the large library case and are scattered on each of the three tables beside the flower-filled vases. The sconces on the back wall are inset with genuine Wedgwood medallions. From the 1760s on, the Wedgwood factory, one of England's most important potteries, produced elegant wares in the Neoclassical style that were immensely popular both in England and abroad.

This room measures 17 × 25 × 34 inches.

Reflecting on the success achieved by the Adam brothers in England during the 1760s and '70s, Mrs. Thorne concluded that one important reason for the popularity of their work was "that they deemed no detail too trivial to receive their personal care." Not only did they design the houses for which they served as architects, but they were also responsible for the complete decoration of the interiors, including all the furniture, mirrors, lighting fixtures, hardware, painted ceilings and wall schemes, carpeting, draperies, and other fabrics. The result was the kind of harmonious elegance well represented by this dining room. Mrs. Thorne modeled the interior after the dining room of Home House in London (1774–78), designed by Robert Adam. The room also incorporates elements from another dining room by the same architect, at Saltram in Devonshire. Robert Adam studied architecture in Italy at a time when the archeological excavations at Pompeii and Herculaneum and at the site of Diocletian's palace in Spalato in Dalmatia stimulated great interest in classical architecture and decoration throughout Europe (see E-25). The delicacy and lightness of his interpretation of the antique, close to the spirit of the Rococo, assured him of enormous success, and his name became forever associated with the style.

In practice in London with his brother James, Robert hired cabinetmakers like Thomas Chippendale, Jr., to execute furniture whose design juxtaposed Neoclassical elements with current English forms. In designing interiors, he replaced wood and wallpapers with paint and plaster, working out most of the ornament in low relief in the manner of Roman stuccos, set against a painted plaster background in framed or unframed panels.

Much of the furniture designed by Adam was gilded in the Continental fashion, as in this interior's side table (the immediate ancestor of the sideboard) and flanking pedestals and in the oval wine cooler underneath. All of these pieces, as well as the two torchères in front of the window, are ornamented with ram's heads, a classical motif that appears in white throughout the frieze of the room. Furniture veneered with light-colored woods such as satinwood and sycamore and often decorated with Neoclassical marquetry or painting—like the two commodes on both sides of the window—was highly fashionable at this time.

The commodes, rug, chandelier, and silver are all taken from Adam designs. The urns on the mantel are copied from examples of Wedgwood. The painting over the mantel is a copy of Claude Lorrain's *Landscape with the Flight into Egypt* in the Gemäldegalerie, Dresden. The landscape opposite is in the style of Claude.

"Robert Adam had many imitators," wrote Mrs. Thorne, "but there was a quality to his work which others aspired to but did not achieve."

This room measures 20 × 35¼ × 25⅝ inches.

11. English Entrance Hall of the Georgian Period, c. 1775

The Adam style influenced the efforts of younger contemporaries, including Thomas Leverton and James Wyatt, elements of whose work are to be found in this interior. Mrs. Thorne had been charmed by "a small house of beautiful proportions," No. 1 Bedford Square, built by Leverton in 1776. The ceiling, plasterwork, floor, and staircase of this hall strongly resemble those in Leverton's house.

The anteroom, with its stenciled arabesque design, is done in the manner of James Wyatt, who frequently reflected the Adams brothers' use of pilasters and sunken panels covered with Etruscan and Pompeian motifs. Painted arabesque decorations had been popular in Italy since the Renaissance, but the extensive archeological activity there in the 18th century led to more careful study of antique originals. The work of such contemporary artist-decorators as Angelica Kauffman and the engraver G. B. Cipriani, as well as a series of major publications on the excavations at Pompeii and Herculaneum, helped popularize this mode of decoration.

The furniture in this hall is based on Neoclassical designs by Robert Adam. The armchairs resemble a gilded Adam-esque example of about 1780, now in the Victoria and Albert Museum. The table in front of the staircase is mod-

eled after a piece depicted in a water-color by Cipriani and reproduced in M. Jourdain's *English Furniture of the Later XVIII Century.*

The circular rug in the entrance, which repeats the design of the dome above, is a typical Adam device. The cameo plaques forming the base of the

candle sconces in the anteroom are miniature examples of Wedgwood jasperware. The winged figure by the front door is of ivory. Facing the front door within the anteroom is a commode flanked by two oval-back armchairs and surmounted by a mirror in a gilded frame. About this room Mrs.

Thorne commented: "Producing in miniature the dainty lunette (above the doorway in the hall) and the iron balustrade was a master stroke in building models of one-inch scale."

The anteroom measures 15¾ × 27 × 4½ inches.

12. English Drawing Room of the Georgian Period, c. 1800

Mrs. Thorne created this interior as a setting for the work of Thomas Sheraton, whom she regarded as having designed "the most exquisite furniture in the history of English mobiliary art." Showing the influence of Adam and his contemporaries in the decoration of the mantelpiece, the slender pilasters above the fireplace, and the moldings, this room was intended to "give the atmosphere of those country villages of late 18th-century England, which were peopled with the hypersensitive women and overindulged and overestimated men whom Jane Austen immortalized."

With the exception of the two side chairs flanking the cabinet, all the furniture is of the Neoclassical type associated with the designs published in 1791 in Sheraton's *Cabinet-maker and Upholsterer's Drawing-Book*. In general, what is referred to as "Sheraton" furniture (before the style came under the influence of the French Empire style [see E-26]) is distinguished by its lightness in weight and color. His designs reveal a penchant for simple shapes combined with either painted or inlaid patterns that are at once elegant and elaborate. Satinwood, sycamore, and other light-colored woods supplemented or replaced mahogany at this time. Satinwood veneers lent themselves to marquetry and to the incorporation of the kind of elegant scroll painting seen on the cabinet against the left wall and on the harpsichord.

The furniture in this interior was made in England. The harpsichord is strung with wires attached to ivory keys that move up and down. A small violin lies in the case on the window seat. The two sconces are made of fine pieces of gilded bronze (ormolu) inset with Wedgwood blue and white jasperware. The hanging shelf holds books and porcelain, including miniature reproductions of figures from the Chelsea porcelain factory. A delicate blue and white tea set rests on the pedestal table before the fireplace. Standing in front of the bay window is a sewing table decorated with marquetry and painting. Through the door to the left is a room furnished with a settee and a screen.

This room measures 11¼ × 19 × 16½ inches.

13. English Rotunda and Library of the Regency Period, 1810–20

"Biographers have laid much stress upon [the prince regent's] amorous proclivities," wrote Mrs. Thorne, "but we must give him credit for other interests. During the long period he was a strong force in England, he certainly set his seal upon the architectural development of London streets, parks, and his royal residences both in London and Brighton."

English architecture and decorative arts during the period when George, Prince of Wales, became regent (he succeeded to the throne as George IV in 1820) were influenced by developments across the channel, where Napoleon was trying to revive the grandeur of Imperial Rome (see E-26). Two of the chief exponents of this style in England were the architects Sir John Soane and Henry Holland. Each man represents two distinct design approaches. Holland, who enjoyed many royal commissions, worked in an elaborate, extravagant manner on such buildings as Carlton House and the original Royal Pavilion at Brighton. Sir John Soane's massively proportioned designs are more restrained. "To illustrate the Regency period at its best," wrote Mrs. Thorne, "I have chosen the hall at Stone House, Lewisham, built by . . . Soane. The dome ceiling, Greek frieze, and marble pillars create an appropriate setting for the echo of French Empire furniture, which distinguished the Regency period."

The built-in bookcase dominating the library is modeled after an original in Kenwood, a famous London residence designed by Robert Adam in 1767. The furniture in the circular hall is meant to be of black lacquer or ebony ornamented with gilded or brass mounts and inlays as well as with variegated exotic hardwoods. The desk and three armchairs in the library illustrate the use of reddish mahogany.

The books have tooled leather bindings. The antique ivory statuettes on the mantel came from what Mrs. Thorne described as "a noted collection of 18th-century bibelots."

The rotunda measures 16 × 22 × 19 inches.

14. English Drawing Room of the Victorian Period, 1840–70

During the 1930s the negative reaction to Victorian taste was so strong that, according to Mrs. Thorne, it was difficult "to obtain accurate information regarding Victorian rooms, for there had been practically nothing written on the subject. Even in England my search was unrewarded."

Admitting to a soft spot for the period, she lavished considerable care on this interior, especially on details.

By this time the Industrial Revolution had made its mark on the design and manufacture of every kind of article for household use. Technological innovations led to quicker and cheaper modes of making furniture, and a growing middle class provided an expanding market for goods that had once been the exclusive preserve of the aristocracy. During the Victorian period the harmonious interiors of the Georgian era gave way to more eclectic settings incorporating a wide range of historical revival styles. This room includes a ceiling with several Renaissance motifs, a mantel and windows inspired by Baroque and Rococo sources, and walls decorated with white Chippendale scrollwork in a Gothic mode.

The deep red carpet and satin curtains elaborately festooned and trimmed with gold silk fringe; the opulent enrichments of black lacquer and gilding on the console tables along the left wall; and the rosewood, walnut, and dark mahogany furniture combine to produce an atmosphere of warmth and comfort, which is what Mrs. Thorne intended. Some of the furniture is from an earlier period. The étagère against the right wall was copied from a piece dating from about 1795 shown in P. Macquoid's *Dictionary of English and French Furniture*. Mrs. Thorne modified its original design by replacing drawers with shelves. The pedestal tables reflect types dating from about 1808.

The pedestal table in front of the center window carries an enamel of Victoria as Dowager Empress and an early photograph of Victoria and her consort, Albert. Married to Victoria in 1840, Albert was named prince consort in 1857; he died four years later. On the pedestal table in the left foreground rests a miniature enameled souvenir book of the coronation, which opens to reveal photographs of the royal family.

The portrait to the left of the window showing Victoria in her coronation robes is a copy of one in the National Portrait Gallery in London painted by Sir George Hayter. The portrait to the right of the window is a copy of Franz Xavier Winterhalter's painting of the prince consort in the National Portrait Gallery, London. Another portrait of Victoria can be glimpsed through the doorway. The two small prints flanking the fireplace are known as Baxter prints, named after the man who developed a mode of printing with oil colors. The one to the left depicts Osborne House, Victoria's country home on the Isle of Wight designed by Prince Albert with the help of architect Thomas Cubitt; the one on the right is of Balmoral Castle in Scotland, completed to Albert's designs in 1856.

This room measures 17½ × 28¼ × 21¾ inches.

15: English Drawing Room of the Modern Period, 1930s

In planning this interior, Mrs. Thorne was free of the constraints of history. She was dealing with her own time and could base her creation on direct observation. "I have followed no school of design," she confessed, "and I have allowed myself complete liberty of expression."

On visits to various London homes, she had admired combinations of old and new, "modernized, simplified backgrounds—fine Georgian mantels and doors undisturbed . . . many interesting uses of mirrors for reflection and brilliance." And she had noted that the "vogue of the hour is Rococo wall treatment with modernized traditional furniture and, here and there, rare antique pieces."

Many of these elements are reflected in this interior. The ornament and color scheme were inspired by a portrait of King Edward VIII, a copy of which hangs over the mantel. Prince-of-Wales plumes and a shell motif form the Rococo design on the gray walls, while the royal blue velvet curtains reflect the color of the king's robes.

Viewed from the perspective of the preceding interiors, this room appears as a contemporary expression of aesthetic standards—correct proportion, restraint, elegance—established in England by such figures as Wren, Adam, and Soane. In its distillation of earlier stylistic elements, the interior expresses the essential conservatism of English design during the first half of the 20th century.

The very simple upholstered sofa and chairs work well with adaptations of 18th-century Chinese Chippendale examples (the chairs and table to the right), the severe interpretation of Rococo plasterwork, the glass and chromium table and screen, and the Venetian blinds. Modern materials reappear in the dining room through the door at the right, where a chromium-topped table on glass legs is set for dinner with contemporary appointments.

Mrs. Thorne had her reservations about "the early packing box type of furniture," as she put it, and rejected the notion of "chairs made of tortured plumbers' pipe, camouflaged with a wash of chromium and upholstered in slippery leather." But she allowed that "when modern furnishings suggest sumptuous simplicity by the use of rich materials and effective coloring, I am keenly enthusiastic." This interior is a clear expression of her enthusiasm.

Through the windows a deep blue night sky sparkles with the lights of Clarence Terrace seen across Regent's Park.

This room measures 17 × 27 × 21 inches.

16. French Hall of the Louis XII Period, c. 1500

To prepare for this interior, Mrs. Thorne toured the Loire Valley, visiting its magnificent châteaux. She was impressed with the grandeur of the château at Blois, birthplace of Louis XII and a favorite residence of later monarchs. Regretting the absence of furniture—"the vital touch," as she called it—at Blois, she had to model the furnishings in this room after pieces she saw at another château in the Loire region, at Langeais, and in the Musée Cluny, Paris.

The Louis XII period was one of transition. As the need for constant vigilance against armed attack decreased, the fortified feudal strongholds evolved into more attractive domiciles. And, while elements of the Gothic style continued to predominate, the influence of the Italian Renaissance became apparent in the furnishings of the châteaux.

The canopied seat, resembling a choir stall, along the left wall and the elaborately carved cupboard or *dressoir* on the opposite wall evoke ecclesiastical furnishings in the late Gothic period. Also medieval in form are the two panel-back chairs flanking the fireplace and the metalwork, particularly the candlestand and lectern in the foreground. The remaining wood pieces are Italian in style. While the many objects in this hall show the variety of furnishings available and the decorative details of the period, such an array of ecclesiastical and domestic pieces is not historically accurate. For example, there would have been few chairs. The chair was not a normal piece of furniture until the Renaissance; before that, people sat on stools.

The fireplace mantel, modeled after one at Chaumont, bears the emblems Mrs. Thorne had noted at Blois: "the symbols of Louis XII and Anne of Brittany—his angry looking porcupine and her delicate little ermine, surmounted by a crown. These were used in the decoration and the carving, just as later Napoleon used the bee and Josephine the swan."

This room measures 22 × 25 × 39¾ inches.

17. French Bedroom, Late 16th Century

"At Azay-le-Rideau," wrote Mrs. Thorne, "I touched and thoroughly examined the piece of old leather, the design of which I have had painted on the walls of the miniature room planned to represent the decorative style of the period of [François I]." The painted and beamed ceiling of this room was inspired by the same source. The overmantel was adapted from one in the château at Loches and depicts a salamander, emblem of François I.

Impressed by the magnificent architecture and decorative and fine arts he had seen on a visit to Italy, François I (reigned 1515–47) undertook an enormous program of château construction, inviting some of Italy's greatest architects and artists—Leonardo da Vinci, Benvenuto Cellini, Primaticcio, and Rosso Fiorentino—to design and decorate such royal residences as Fontainebleau and Chambord.

Like the Louis XII hall (E-16), this room contains more cabinets and seat furniture than would have been included in an actual bedchamber. Despite its inaccuracies, this interior conveys a sense of the splendor that Mrs. Thorne associated with the luxury-loving and extravagant king. Most of the furnishings reflect styles dating from the second half of the 16th or early part of the 17th century. The exceptions are the two Gothic joint stools (one next to the bed, the other in the right foreground) and the panel-back chair near the 17th-century-style draped bed. The stools, it should be noted, would not have served as tables. The two cabinets, called *armoires-à-deux-corps,* and the high-back carved chair were copied from originals in the Musée Cluny.

The portrait miniature on the left wall, of a later period, came from an antique collection in Brittany, as did the small reliquary and rosary to the right of the bed, and the gold ornaments on the oak credence. The chandelier was made from small pieces of gilded bronze (ormolu) found in a shop in Paris.

Through the open door one sees a simulated tapestry; the window to the left affords a glimpse of the town of Loches.

This room measures 19¼ × 26 × 27 inches.

18. French Salon of the Louis XIV Period, 1660–1700

During the period of Louis XIV, the Sun King (reigned 1643–1715), France became the dominant political and cultural force in Europe. In the course of his long reign the king availed himself of the services of many of Europe's finest artists, architects, designers, and craftsmen to create a grand manner that would express the glory of his rule. They adapted architectural and decorative forms of the Italian High Renaissance and Baroque styles to grand decorating schemes that encompassed all the arts. The most monumental and ambitious of these was, of course, the royal palace at Versailles.

Mrs. Thorne decided to devote two rooms to this significant period. "The first room," she explained, "is designed to show the magnificence expressed in decorative design during the early part of the reign. . . . It is a salon in which Le Grand Monarque would have received his nobles. [For it] I have selected the architectural style of Jean Le Pautre, with great pilasters, massive doors, tall windows and niches holding statuary. . . . The ceiling of this room shows the continued Italian influence." Jean Le Pautre was one of the creators of what became known as the Louis XIV style. Le Pautre's more than 2,000 engravings of architectural and decorative details—from ceilings and sculptural chimney pieces to elaborately carved furniture—helped disseminate the Grand Manner throughout Europe.

In this interior the gilded furniture, with its elaborate scrolls and carvings, exhibits a continuing Italian influence. The two commodes are copies of pieces in the Wallace Collection, London. They are in the style of André Charles Boulle, the first in the line of eminent French-born designers and furniture makers to work at the French court. The table in the center of the room is modeled after a piece now in the Musée du Louvre, Paris. The painting above the fireplace is a miniature reproduction of Hyacinthe Rigaud's portrait (Louvre) of Louis XIV in his robes of state. The initial letter of the king's name appears in the room as a decorative motif, as does his emblem, a head surrounded by sun rays. The pile carpet was inspired by those made at the Savonnerie manufactory founded by Louis XIII in 1627. The tapestry that can be seen through the doorway is a copy of one commissioned by the king and executed by tapestry weavers at the royal Gobelins manufactory.

Mrs. Thorne commented on the woeful lack of chairs in the interiors of this period, noting that ladies of the nobility, forced to stand for hours at receptions, often were carried out in a faint, while those who were royal enough to sit in the presence of the king suffered on uncomfortable little stools. She concluded: "The important

looking armchairs associated with this period . . . might almost be called thrones because of the distinction their use conferred."

This room measures 18¾ × 31 × 23¾ inches.

19. French Dining Room of the Louis XIV Period, 1660–1700

For her second Louis XIV room, Mrs. Thorne chose what she described as "more homelike and livable models." These were meant to represent the tastes of "a class of educated and cultured men of letters and of the arts who preferred to have their homes express dignity and simplicity" rather than the extravagance of the court circles.

One source of inspiration for this room was the Paris residence of Madame de Sévigné, known for her witty letters. Mrs. Thorne had visited the home, which had been turned into a museum, and when she came to design this interior she noted, "In such a room as this you can imagine Madame [de] Sévigné entertaining her guests at dinner, in the stiff high-back chairs." Another source was the designs of Jules Hardouin Mansart, which were characteristic of the latter half of the 17th century. The simplicity and relative severity of the oak-paneled interior provide a restrained setting for the gilding and colorful inlays of the furniture, the velvet-brocade upholstery, and the rich hangings.

The high-back chairs, inlaid commode, mirror, and pedestals were inspired by examples in the Musée des Arts Décoratifs, Paris. The side table and table were modeled after designs by Jean Le Pautre (see E-18). The pile effect of Savonnerie carpeting was achieved by substituting wool for silk in the embroidering of the rug. Its design repeats, in part, the central element of the ceiling. The tapestry over the side table was originally part of an antique purse. The gold service displayed on the side table came from one of Mrs. Thorne's secret sources, which she described as "a small shop in Paris which specializes in minute things."

The painting over the side table is a reproduction of a portrait of Cardinal Richelieu by Philippe de Champaigne in the Musée du Louvre.

This room measures 17 × 26½ × 21⅝ inches.

20. French Library of the Louis XV Period, c. 1720

In 1715 the five-year-old great grandson of Louis XIV succeeded to the throne as Louis XV, with Philippe, Duke of Orleans, appointed as regent. The eight years of the regency were ones of significant shifts in French taste in architecture and in the decorative arts, a transition from the classical Baroque style that characterizes the palace of Versailles to the less grandiose and lighter Rococo, which became dominant during the second quarter of the 18th century.

At this time a number of *hôtels particuliers* (townhouses) were built in Paris and their interiors decorated with complex scrollwork combined with shell forms, flowers, ribbons, and other artifices in fanciful arrangements. "Everything must be curves, a revolt against the stiff and uncomfortable lines of Louis XIV," wrote Mrs. Thorne. Régence curves appear in this interior in the overdoor and overpanel decoration, with their painted floral insets. Oak paneling of the kind used here could be either painted or unpainted, with gilding reserved for the ornamentation. With its graceful, flowing lines, the elegant writing table in front of the doorway to the right is typical of the period. The wood of the chairs was usually painted or gilded, while the tables and commodes (such as those along the right wall) were veneered in exotic woods and accented with elaborate ormolu mounts.

The miniature paintings and portraits are in the style of François Boucher. The Boucher composition over the mantel is *Pastoral Subject* in the Musée du Louvre. Originally used as a seal, the bronze bust on the console to the left depicts the philosopher Voltaire. Mrs. Thorne was particularly proud of the fine leather tooling on the books displayed in this library and of the miniature gold coffee set on the pedestal table by the settee which she had acquired in Paris. The placement of the furniture is not typical of the period, but Mrs. Thorne succeeded in conveying her notion of what was appealing about French interiors of this time. "This room is restful and luxurious," she noted.

This room measures 18¼ × 21⅞ × 25⅛ inches.

21. French Boudoir of the Louis XV Period, 1740–60

In planning this interior, Mrs. Thorne wished to suggest the growing concern for comfort in the 18th century. "Due to a desire for luxury and intimacy," she wrote, "rooms were reduced to a reasonable size, methods of heating were improved, and bathrooms and dressing rooms were introduced." Mrs. Thorne attributed these innovations to "the delicate hand of a discerning woman . . . Madame de Pompadour." Though Mrs. Thorne may have overstated the case, Louis XV's mistress did, in fact, exert a great influence on the arts, as she did on the king.

It is not surprising that this period witnessed a proliferation of forms on which to sit and recline, such as the chaise longue (in the foreground on the left), bergère (upholstered armchair with rounded back, wide seat, and upholstery between arm and seat), armchairs, and settee in this room. These pieces combined elegance with comfort, their generous width being well suited to accommodate the voluminous skirts of stiff brocade worn by the ladies of the court. The chaise longue in particular, Mrs. Thorne pointed out, "offered the tightly laced beauties of the day as much relaxation as their corseted figures would permit."

Also typical is the profusion of small cabinets and tables of the kind used in this interior. Often equipped with elaborate opening and closing mechanisms, such pieces were kept small so they could easily be moved about. Appropriate to a boudoir were dressing tables like the one by the window, a necessity in a period of elaborate toilettes and coiffures.

Lighter tones in woods, draperies, and paints became the fashion, with muted colors—rose, lilac, powder blue, and apple green—replacing the deeper shades. The ornamentation at the top and bottom of the paneling in this room is representative of the finely carved clusters of scroll, shell, and floral forms that characterize the Rococo.

The portraits on the back wall are of Louis XV and his queen, Marie Leszczynska. They flank a simulated tapestry, a piece of petit point from one of the antique stores Mrs. Thorne frequented in Paris. Such stores were also the source of the miniature accessories in gold, ivory, and porcelain displayed in this elegant room.

This room measures 18¼ × 24¾ × 23⅛ inches.

22. French Provincial Bedroom of the Louis XV Period, 18th Century

"This bedroom of a country house in Normandy represents the provincial interpretation of the style of Louis XV," wrote Mrs. Thorne. She intended this interior to show the way in which a growing middle class outside of Paris assimilated to their more modest homes some of the innovations in comfort and style characteristic of Louis XV's reign.

A striving for beauty is demonstrated in the richly carved armoire against the left wall and in the sprigged wallpaper supplementing the paneling of the back wall. Wallpaper printed by hand from wooden blocks had been in use in England since the 16th century; in France it became fashionable in the early 18th century. By the 1770s wallpaper designed and made in France was much in vogue.

The curtains and chair coverings are examples of what was then a new process, the decoration of cotton by the use of engraved copper plates. First employed in England in the 1750s, the technique was introduced into France in the 1770s by a manufacturer who established his factory in the town of Jouy—hence the name of the product, "toiles de Jouy." The curtains draped over the alcove enclosing the bed were functional: at night they were closed tightly to keep out drafts.

Mrs. Thorne decorated the room with pictures, faïence ware, and small ornaments acquired during a tour of seacoast towns in Normandy and Brittany. Her observations on the tour led her to add the various objects of religious significance. "These rooms al-

ways reflect the devout character of a seafaring people," she wrote. "You usually find a statue of the Virgin, a prie-dieu, and a crucifix." About this room she wrote touchingly, "There is a quality of homelike comfort permeating these rustic rooms which gives you a sense of peace. . . . While working in my studios, at times the irritations and

problems took away the joy of the task. When I found myself overtired and quite fed-up I would uncover the little Normandy bedroom and mentally creep in to find the peace of simple surroundings."

This room measures 11 × 19½ × 17½ inches.

23. French Dining Room of the Periods of Louis XV and Louis XVI, 1760–80

The last 15 years of Louis XV's reign saw a reaction against the opulent curves and excessive ornamentation of the Rococo in favor of the more sober, rational Neoclassical style. Both in architecture and in the decorative arts, there was a return to simplicity and restraint. Inspired by renewed interest in classical antiquity, this trend continued through the reign of Louis XVI (1774–93) and Marie Antoinette.

Mrs. Thorne viewed the Louis XVI style as reflecting the taste of the queen rather than the king, commenting that "It was his charming and vivacious queen who became the arbiter of decorative design during their reign. She commissioned the architects, artists, and modistes of France to express her fantasies and she created a distinctly feminine style which, paradoxically, is always referred to as Louis XVI."

Two sources are given as the inspiration for this dining room. One is a room in one of the smaller houses in Fontainebleau; the other is the Petit Trianon at Versailles. Mrs. Thorne planned this room "much in the manner of the salons of the Trianon, with tall doors, elaborate carving over them, and the typical marble mantel with the overmirror." Although Mrs. Thorne identified the Trianon with the taste of Marie Antoinette (see E-24), this exquis-itely proportioned building was actually designed and built as a hideaway for Louis XV's powerful mistress, Madame de Pompadour.

Off-white or greenish-gray walls relieved by gilded ornaments and moldings were favored schemes of decoration. The classic simplicity of the walls and panels is echoed in the lines of the furniture, though there is an abundance of fine carving. The design of the table is not of the period. At this time a small, round table would have been customary, with more than one used when necessary. Moreover, it would not have been situated in the center of the room. The placement of the commodes on either side of the fireplace and of the terracotta busts on the side tables is similarly inaccurate for the period. The needlepoint rug is in the style of the delicately textured, smooth-faced tapestry-woven carpets produced in the royal factory at Aubusson. The porcelain vases, gold table service, and mantel ornaments were found by Mrs. Thorne in Paris. The chandelier is festooned with myriads of sparkling crystal beads collected from a variety of sources.

This room measures 19¼ × 31¾ × 22⅜ inches.

24. French Salon of the Louis XVI Period, c. 1780

Mrs. Thorne designed this interior "entirely in the spirit of Marie Antoinette—dainty in coloring and full of her symbols of design." The queen was fond of roses, which were often incorporated into the molded decorations of swags, garlands, and baskets in rooms such as this one. Peach-colored roses also dot the curtains here. The garden tools and musical instruments in the carvings of the panel heads represent her love of nature and music.

The marquetry commode and secretary with marble tops and drawers that actually can be opened and locked with tiny keys are antique pieces found in Paris by Mrs. Thorne. The armchair, lyre-back chair, and settee were modeled after 18th-century examples in the Musée des Arts Décoratifs; the side chairs were copied from G. Henriot's *Les Beaux Meubles des collections privées* and S. de Ricci's *Louis XVI Furniture.* These reproductions were delicately carved and upholstered in silk or fine needlepoint suggestive of Beauvais tapestry. The majority of the chairs in this period would have been painted rather than gilded. On the walls are antique miniatures from Paris painted on ivory, in the style of famed 18th-century painters Jean Baptiste Greuze and Jean Honoré Fragonard. The bust in the right corner is said to depict Marie Antoinette.

Mrs. Thorne had a special feeling for the pleasure-loving queen, whose life ended tragically during the French Revolution. Speaking of the Petit Trianon, whose private rooms inspired this salon, she wrote, "Nothing could be more chaste, more restrained. This was Marie Antoinette's favorite retreat and it is here that I always feel her shadow."

This room measures 15 × 20½ × 17 inches.

In 1792 the French monarchy was abolished. Three years later the National Assembly was replaced by the Directorate. The succeeding decade saw the rise to power of Napoleon Bonaparte. He became consul in 1799 and in 1804 was crowned emperor.

This interior reflects the republican phase of the Directorate and Consulate, during which the ancient Roman symbols of republicanism were incorporated into the idiom of decoration. Many of the classical elements in such rooms, like the sunken circular bathtub and skylight (oculus) above, the decorative panels, the furniture, as well as the colors—earth reds, yellows, and blacks—were inspired by the frescoes, mosaics, and objects uncovered in the excavations of Pompeii and Herculaneum earlier in the century.

Mrs. Thorne intended these rooms to represent the tumultuous changes that characterize this period: "Everything must be different. . . . Furniture forms became simple, modified with classical symbols such as crossed arrows, lyres, and laurel wreaths. Draperies of plain materials in strong, pure colors were hung over poles in severe folds. . . . It was an interesting period proclaiming . . . the new idea of 'Liberty, Equality, Fraternity.' "

This attachment to republican simplicity did not last long, she noted, because "there are always new rich who want to display their wealth, and such architects as [François Joseph] Bélanger were soon building exquisite houses and designing elaborate interiors."

Mrs. Thorne used as the inspiration of these rooms a portfolio of Bélanger's watercolor renderings for a commission that she found at the Musée des Arts Décoratifs.

The bathroom furniture is meant to be of fruitwood and ebony. The gilded candle brackets have been embellished with a lyre and swans (later, Empress Josephine adopted the swan as her emblem). The painted pieces in the bedroom, like the inset panels in the bathroom, reflect a Pompeian influence. Bélanger had visited England and was an admirer of Robert Adam, who had made Neoclassicism fashionable in England (see E-10). Ivory miniatures of Napoleon and Josephine are set on the table in front of the window as is a miniature metal statue of the future emperor.

The bathroom measures 13⅞ × 23 × 12¾ inches.

26. French Anteroom of the Empire Period, c. 1810

Napoleon's taste as emperor gravitated toward a lavish, elaborate, archeologically correct version of Neoclassicism identified with Imperial Rome, which came to be known as the Empire style. Its chief practitioners in Paris were Charles Percier and Pierre François Léonard Fontaine, who had come to Napoleon's notice when they redecorated the château at Malmaison in which he and Josephine lived from 1800 to 1803. The two architects not only designed buildings, rooms, furnishings, textiles, and silver, but also staged such events as Napoleon's coronation and his wedding to his second wife, Marie Louise of Austria.

In this room Mrs. Thorne was inspired by the designs of Percier and Fontaine, as well as Bélanger: "I chose this octagonal hall because of the stately severity of its lines, which seem to embody the spirit of imperialism. It lacks [a] livable quality, but it is 100 percent Napoleonic, and that is what I was striving for."

The influence of Imperial Rome is revealed in the treatment of the wall surfaces to suggest marble veneer on a core of brick masonry and in the ornament simulating gilded bronze applied to the marble surface. The ornament is typical of the work of Percier and Fontaine, who often incorporated emblems associated with Napoleon—the Imperial eagle, the bee, the laurel wreath, or the initial N—into their designs for draperies and furnishings.

After Napoleon's Egyptian campaign, French architects, according to Mrs. Thorne, "indulged in a perfect orgy of Egyptian design," here represented by the use of the sphinx as a motif in the table, chairs, and fireplace decoration.

Bolder colors became fashionable during this period. Typical color schemes included gold on black or mahogany red in furniture, gold on crimson damask in upholstery and drapery, and gold on rich brown in rugs, with blue or green often used in place of the red. The curtains and the silk on the chairs in this room are of a green color known in Mrs. Thorne's time as "Empire." The niche is painted in what was called Pompeian red.

The miniature sculpture in the niche was purchased in Pompeii and depicts Narcissus. The bust of Napoleon on the mantel at one time served as the top of a bell. The rug, both in color and pattern, was copied from a cartoon that was part of a portfolio of designs for rugs that Napoleon commissioned for Fontainebleau.

This room measures 17¼ × 29½ × 19½ inches.

27. French Library of the Modern Period, 1930s

Rather than emulating a particular interior, this room combines elements of several styles developed in the decade following World War I in such centers of modern design and craftsmanship as Paris, Berlin, and Vienna. The setting conveys a sense of affluence and cultivation, of the 1937 Paris Exposition Universelle with its celebration of progress and modernity, and of the French colonial presence in Indochina.

Commenting that "modern French decoration has a very broad scope of ideas and types," Mrs. Thorne created a streamlined architectural setting, whose modernity is accented by the sweeping curve of the wall to the right. The woodwork is bleached to a pale tone so as to provide, as she explained, "an effective background for [the] ornate Chinese ornament so much appreciated in France."

The Oriental influence is evident in the neutral tones of the fabrics and accessories, in the two side chairs inspired by bamboo originals, in the black lacquer table, and in the Chinese brocade upholstery of the banquette and matching tub chairs, whose broad, stylized character recalls 1920s Art-Deco design. Oriental accents are also found in the gilded Buddha, the carnelian bowls on the shelf behind the banquette, and the Khmer head on the pedestal.

The Cubistic cityscapes flanking the fireplace are petit-point tapestries reflecting, in Mrs. Thorne's words, "the new type of designs being done by a famous school of needlework in Vienna."

The center doorway leads onto a formal rooftop garden arranged around a modernist sculpture of a half-nude female figure. The doorway to the right opens onto an iron-railed balcony on which a table has been set for breakfast. From this vantage point unfolds a dramatic panorama of Paris, with the Eiffel Tower visible in the distance.

This room measures 16⅛ × 24⅜ × 19½ inches.

28. German Sitting Room of the "Biedermeier" Period, 1815–50

Between 1855 and 1857 a German writer named Ludwig Eichrodt published satiric verses about Papa Biedermeier, a fictitious figure who expressed the foibles and ambivalences of the German middle class. Papa Biedermeier became the symbol of the common man and his name came to be associated with the atmosphere and decor of an earlier period—the decades following the defeat of Napoleon in 1815.

The Napoleonic conquest had spread throughout the Continent the heady mixture of egalitarian principles proclaimed by the French Revolution and the grandiose pretensions of Napoleon's short-lived empire. A postwar reaction against the grand character of the Empire style prompted the development of the Biedermeier style of furniture, which is above all functional, solid, and comfortable. "The simple and provincial character of [Biedermeier] furniture," wrote Mrs. Thorne, "shows the protest of the German middle class against the sumptuousness of the Napoleonic era."

Mrs. Thorne based this interior on a portfolio of twenty-four color plates, from which she chose two that seemed to her to "give a good idea of the spirit of Biedermeier." The plain woodwork, painted and papered walls, and elaborate borders are characteristic of the style, as are the festooned and fringed draperies.

In keeping with furniture designs of the period, the pieces, for the most part, reflect the use of pale wood—pear, ash, mahogany, cherry, or birch—with strong accents of ebonized black. Early Biedermeier seating pieces tended to have curved legs and backs, a feature often repeated in other forms. As the years went by, the relative restraint of the ornamentation, confined to pilasters and columns, yielded to greater embellishment.

Through the door on the right is a bedchamber. Mrs. Thorne claimed that the yellow bonnet on the stand next to the bed provided the initial inspiration for this room. There was, however, another source: a watercolor of the living room of the Baroness Munch-Bellinghausen, reproduced in J. A. Lux's *Empire und Biedermeier.* The tiled stove in the marbelized niche, the commode, floor, wallpaper border, type of chandelier, and arrangement of pictures in Mrs. Thorne's model bear a strong resemblance to their counterparts in this illustration. This tends to confirm one's suspicion that Mrs. Thorne's interior was aristocratic, after all, and would have been somewhat beyond the means of a Papa Biedermeier.

"My model of a Biedermeier room may seem overcrowded with furniture and ornaments," wrote Mrs. Thorne, "and the walls may appear too cluttered with pictures. But truly, what seems overdecoration is hardly sufficient to represent the exuberant taste of this charming . . . style."

This room measures 14⅝ × 21 × 21¼ inches.

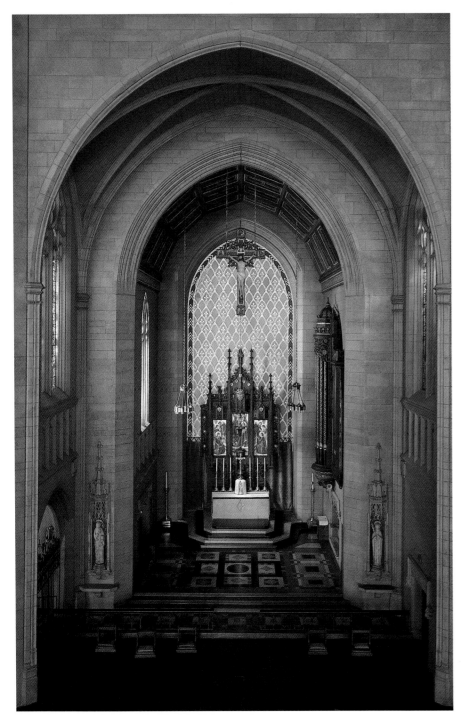

29. English Roman Catholic Church in the Gothic Style, Late 13th Century

This model, designated by Mrs. Thorne as Our Lady Queen of Angels Church, is unusual in a number of respects. To begin with, it is designed on a slightly smaller scale than the preceding interiors — three-quarters of an inch rather than one inch to the foot. In describing this interior, Mrs. Thorne stressed the functions of the various elements rather than presenting its historical context. And, quite uncharacteristically, she concluded her account by naming the architect, artists, and craftsmen who created the model. Mrs. Thorne asked the architect Elliott L. Chisling of New York to design an English church in the style of the period before Gothic ornament "became flamboyant and decadent." The result illustrates a phase of English Gothic some-

where between the High Gothic style of the 13th century and the Perpendicular style of the 14th century.

However, Mrs. Thorne's church exhibits some un-Gothic features — the vaulted ceiling above the sanctuary (the part of the church that contains the altar) is paneled in wood coffers. And a decorated wall replaces the customary east window above the reredos, the wooden screen that enfolds the painted altarpiece.

The elaborately carved reredos, inspired by models in English cathedrals, was executed by Alfons Weber, a Chicago craftsman who also carved the crucifix. The altar is freestanding, raised three steps above the sanctuary floor. On the right side of the altar is a credence intended to house the instruments of the sacraments and a sedile (official chair). A piscina (basin) is built into the masonry of the wall. Above the doorway leading to the priest's chamber, or sacristy, rise the pipes of the organ. The organ console stands in a niche of the wall to the left of the altar under the window. The adjacent door leads into the vestry, so called because the vestments (and sometimes the sacred vessels) were stored there.

A wrought-iron grille in a 15th-century style screens the entrance to the chapel dedicated to the Sacred Heart in the left bay. The grille, altar fittings, and lighting fixtures were the work of a New York artist, Marie Zimmerman. Hildreth Meiere, also of New York, executed the murals and polychroming; and another New Yorker, G. Owen Bonawit, a well-known artist who worked in glass, designed and painted the windows. Chicagoan Lawrence Brom of the Francis Kramer Studios constructed the model;

and A. W. Pederson, also of Chicago, painted the walls, ceiling, and elaborate floor design.

Mrs. Thorne noted the absence of pews, "which are modern comforts" first introduced in the 16th century. The only furnishings in the nave (the main body of the church between the aisles) are prayer stands.

This room measures 48 × 32½ × 41½ inches.

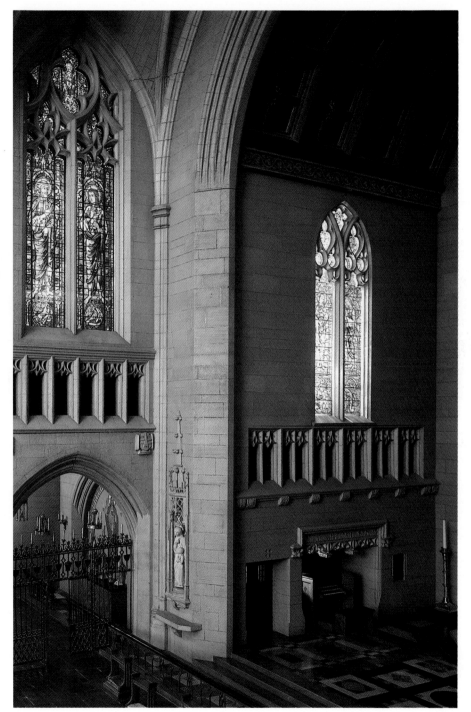

30. Chinese Interior, Traditional

While many of the European Rooms were based on interiors that Mrs. Thorne saw and admired on her trips to England and France, this Chinese setting appears to have been created on the basis of literary sources. The style depicted here is one that evolved over the course of more than 2,000 years. Although the Western commercial presence was well established in several Chinese cities by the end of the 19th century, few Europeans or Americans would have had direct contact with the prosperous upper-class Chinese who occupied homes like this one. The style of life led within such traditional Chinese settings was to be severely affected by the upheavals of World War II, the subsequent civil war, and the establishment of the People's Republic of China.

In building their houses the Chinese followed traditional, fixed plans. While house types differed from region to region, most were organized around central courtyards that provided light and air to the surrounding rooms. The important rooms faced south and were flanked to the east and west by subsidiary rooms of identical size and shape.

This rigid symmetry in the arrangement of the spaces created a desired sense of balance, order, and peace.

Such qualities are evident in the reception room depicted here. The interior is divided into two halves that are, in turn, separated into smaller areas by wooden screens. Centered on the back wall, an ancestral portrait hangs over a table on which are displayed candlesticks and decorative porcelains. In the middle space family treasures would have been stored in pieces like the decorated chests on either side of the doorway. The foreground contains the main area, which would have opened onto the courtyard. Reinforcing the room's symmetry are the wooden screens, with their elaborately carved panels and fretwork. The traditional material for most Chinese buildings was wood, used not only for structural elements but also as elegant decoration.

To the left of the main area is a sitting room furnished with a carved teakwood couch and armchair upholstered in rich brocade, and a chest. To the right is a bedroom containing a bed, dressing table, washstand, and full-length mirror set in a carved wooden frame. Both rooms display hanging painted scrolls. Throughout the interior the elaborately carved teakwood and lacquer furniture is arranged symmetrically in formal groupings.

The foreground room measures 12¼ × 21¾ × 13 inches.

31. Japanese Interior, Traditional

In their traditional domestic architecture the Japanese characteristically use wooden panels and paper shutters as the chief building materials for the exterior, and fixed or sliding panels of wood and rice paper as dividers in the interior. Such dividers offer the convenience of flexibility in the arrangement of the interior space. To represent Japanese architecture, Mrs. Thorne chose the *zashiki,* or main room, of the traditional Japanese home and the adjoining room customarily used by the mistress of the house.

Essential elements of the main room are the two recessed areas at the back. The alcove to the left houses artistically arranged wall cabinets and shelves for art objects. The alcove to the right is traditionally used to display a single work of art—a scroll or vase—chosen to be enjoyed for the day from a stock of such treasures kept in a fireproof storeroom. The floor of the main room is always covered with *tatami,* or straw mats, each of which measures about three by six feet and is bound with cotton borders.

The simple and harmonious structure of Japanese architecture is apparent in spite of the somewhat excessive number of objects Mrs. Thorne placed in the room. The translucent *shoji* (sliding doors) which give easy access to the garden at the right and the floral motifs

painted on the sliding doors that divide the *zashiki* from the room at the left, integrate the architecture with the natural setting outside. In the room at the left three kimonos hang over a traditional stand, and the articles necessary for a woman's toilette await use on the low table. The mirror and stand were made out of alloyed metal specifically for this model by a Japanese artist.

The absence of furnishings other than the lacquer writing desk and low tables in the main room is typical. Other accessories, including bedding, are brought into a room as the occasion demands. The writing desk in the *zashiki,* the screen in the adjoining room, and the stone ornaments in the garden are among several objects in this interior modeled after items depicted in E. S. Morse's *Japanese Homes and Their Surroundings.*

This room measures 10½ × 23¼ × 15½ inches.

AMERICAN ROOMS

1. Massachusetts Living Room and Kitchen, 1675—1700
2. New Hampshire Parlor, c. 1710
3. Massachusetts Dining Room, 1720
4. Connecticut Valley Tavern Parlor, c. 1750
5. Massachusetts Drawing Room, 1768
6. New Hampshire Dining Room, 1760
7. New Hampshire Entrance Hall, 1799
8. Massachusetts Bedroom, c. 1801
9. Massachusetts Parlor, 1818
10. Massachusetts Dining Room, 1795
11. Rhode Island Parlor, c. 1820
12. Cape Cod Living Room, 1750—1850
13. New England Bedroom, 1750—1850
14. Pennsylvania Drawing Room, 1834—36
15. New York City Parlor, 1850—70
16. Pennsylvania Drawing Room, 1761
17. Pennsylvania Kitchen, 1752
18. Shaker Living Room, c. 1800
19. Maryland Dining Room, 1770—74
20. Virginia Dining Room, 1758
21. Virginia Parlor, 1758—87
22. Virginia Dining Room, c. 1752
23. Virginia Drawing Room, 1754
24. Virginia Entrance Hall, 1751—55
25. Virginia Drawing Room, 1755
26. Virginia Dining Room, c. 1800
27. Virginia Kitchen, 18th Century
28. South Carolina Drawing Room, 1775—1800
29. South Carolina Ballroom, 1775—1835
30. Georgia Double Parlor, c. 1850
31. Tennessee Entrance Hall, 1835
32. Louisiana Bedroom, 1800—50
33. "Middletown" Parlor, 1875—1900
34. New Mexico Dining Room, c. 1940
35. California Living Room, c. 1935—40
36. California Living Room, 1850—75
37. California Hallway, c. 1940

These items, drawn from the American miniature rooms, are pictured in their actual sizes based on a scale of one inch to a foot. The coffee urn and stand are from Room A-20; the armchair from A-10; the sideboard and silver from A-22; and the rug from A-31.

1. Massachusetts Living Room and Kitchen, 1675–1700

This interior represents a domestic setting of some 50 years after the Pilgrims had established their settlement at Plymouth. By this time, the relatively primitive shelters of woven boughs and mud built by the first permanent settlers in North America had given way to more substantial houses resembling those left behind in England, but made of local materials and adapted to local use. In this, as in the following interiors, the settlers' attachment to the familiar is clear. English models would remain the dominant influence on architecture and furnishings for a long time to come.

In creating this interior Mrs. Thorne turned to two models—a room from Parson Capen's house built in 1683 in Topsfield, Massachusetts, and a period room displayed by the Concord (Massachusetts) Antiquarian Society. In this kind of combined kitchen and living room, the fireplace played a crucial role, serving as the sole means both of heating and cooking. The baking oven built into the thick brickwork and the iron cooking pot on the crane were supplemented by a variety of utensils of the sort grouped around the mantel and grate. Sturdy wooden bowls and trenchers and pewter plates and mugs tended to be used rather than pottery and glass, by now fairly common in England. Kitchen floors were usually covered with sand, which, when swept out, took the refuse with it. Though the first kinds of rugs recorded in the colony were braided ones like those used by Mrs. Thorne in this interior, they would have been rare at this time.

The walls of this room are sheathed in pine—a local wood. Windows were few and small because of the high cost

of glass. Ceilings were low to conserve heat. The furnishings of this room are somewhat more abundant than was common at the time. Some pieces might have been brought from England, but most of the benches, chests, stools, and settles were made locally. The settle's high back, which extends all the way to the floor, was designed to protect the sitter from drafts. Stools like the ones grouped around the fireplace were more common than chairs, which were rare at the time. An armchair, or "great chair," as it was called, was considered a seat of honor. The two in this room are models of types that in Mrs. Thorne's day acquired the names of historical figures from the Colonial period. To the left stands a Governor Carver chair; to the right, fashioned of many spindles, is an Elder Brewster chair. The originals were made between 1640 and 1660. The miniature ship on the mantel is a model of the *Mayflower*. Mrs. Thorne placed an antique painted doll in the child's chair to the right of the fireplace.

Through the door can be glimpsed a bedroom with a folding press bed and a trundle bed, both copied from W. Nutting's *Furniture Treasury* and both from the 18th rather than the 17th century. Bedrooms of this period were sparsely furnished—with a large bed, cradle, and trundle bed on wheels for the older children. During the day the trundle bed would be stored under the big bed.

This room measures 8⅝ × 18⅛ × 14 inches.

2. New Hampshire Parlor, c. 1710

The last years of the 17th century and early years of the 18th were a time of rapidly increasing prosperity and comfort for the citizens of the New England colonies. To illustrate the transformation of homes that catered to necessities into ones that offered greater amenities, Mrs. Thorne chose to reproduce the parlor of the Samuel Wentworth home in Portsmouth, installed at The Metropolitan Museum of Art, New York, under the designation "John Wentworth House," John being Samuel's son.

Built in 1671, the house was remodeled extensively in 1710, by which time the paneled wall and double-hung windows were part of the room upon which this interior is based. Paneling encompassing an opening for a fireplace became a common feature of 18th-century American houses, inspired by English models. This was also the case with double-hung windows (in which the sashes slide up and down the frame), which first came into use in England during the late 16th and early 17th centuries.

English influence can also be seen in the furnishings of this interior. The press cupboard, copied from an original believed to have been made near Boston between 1660 and 1680, recalls English Jacobean pieces of heavy oak like those depicted in Room E-2. The American cabinetmaker who created the original of this piece substituted split-spindle ornamentation for the tra-

ditional Jacobean carving. The joined chair, with its decoratively carved panel, to the left of the fireplace, was also copied from an American-made version of an English original dating from between 1650 and 1675. The stool, side chair, and day bed (or chaise longue) resemble English Restoration pieces, though in America, where they were popular in the early 18th century, their style is described as William and Mary

(see E-4). Mrs. Thorne modeled the chest and writing box standing between the windows after pieces illustrated in the *Handbook of the Concord Antiquarian Society*.

The chandelier and wrought-iron candlestands are modeled after originals from a house in Rockport, Massachusetts, dating from about 1682 and illustrated in L. V. Lockwood's *Colonial Furniture in America*. The curtains feature an Indian pattern of a type popular during this period. Such patterns were

painted, dyed, or block-printed onto cloth to be used for bedspreads, table covers, and curtains. The small chair next to the center table is covered with what was known as "Turkey work" embroidery, which enjoyed considerable popularity in England during the 17th century. The stoneware pots on the cupboard and by the fireplace reflect examples from a later period. Arranged on the table are a Bible which can actu-

ally be read, a pair of eyeglasses, and a piece of knitting on ivory needles the size of a pin.

A staircase typical of the time can be seen in the hallway through the door on the left.

This room measures 8½ × 22¾ × 16⅛ inches.

3. Massachusetts Dining Room, 1720

More sophisticated than the preceding interior in terms of its architecture and furnishings, this early 18th-century dining room was based on a 1720s addition to the historic Turner-Ingersoll residence built in Salem in 1668. Nathaniel Hawthorne used this house as the setting for his novel *The House of the Seven*

Gables, published in 1851. A fishing town, Salem soon became a shipbuilding center, supplying many of the ships of the great whaling fleets that plied the waters off the Newfoundland Banks when the whaling industry developed after the 1750s.

The shipbuilding industry created many highly skilled shipwrights who,

with guidance from such English manuals as the *Builder's Companion* and *The Young Carpenter's Assistant,* constructed sturdy houses. Although the Turner-Ingersoll house was built in the 17th century, the dining room was added in the early 18th century. Most striking is the paneling, which, instead of being confined to one wall as in the New Hampshire parlor (A-2), is carried around the whole room as far as the chair rail, creating a dado. The pilasters, arched doorway, and cupboard add touches of elegance to the room, as do the paneled window embrasures extending all the way to the floor. It was not uncommon for such decorative woodwork to be added to the rooms of more primitive, earlier houses.

The English influence continued to be very strong during this time; often it would have been difficult to tell which of the pieces in rooms like this had been made in England and which had been built locally. Most of the furniture in a room of this period would have been in what is known as the William and Mary style (see A-2), though the chairs around the gate-leg table are in the later Queen Anne style (see E-6). Gate-leg, trestle-base tables were of English origin but were copied by American craftsmen, who often used cherry for such pieces. The inlaid walnut side table on the left and the high chest of drawers and tall case clock against the right wall were modeled after American pieces made in English

styles of the late 17th century. The chairs with split-baluster backs standing against the walls are distinctly American, as is the banister-back armchair beside the fireplace. Mrs. Thorne copied the latter, identified as dating from the first quarter of the 18th century, from one depicted in L. V. Lockwood's *Colonial Furniture in America.* The settee and the crewelwork draperies that can be glimpsed through the door on the right were also fashioned after New England models.

Chinese porcelains of the kind displayed in this room first reached America by way of England. Direct American trade with China did not be-

gin until after the Revolution, when the ship *Empress of China* left New York for Canton in 1784 to carry back to North America the first cargo from the Orient. The floor is covered with a reproduction of a Chinese rug like those Salem's merchant captains would have brought back somewhat later, when their whaling voyages took them to the Pacific.

This room measures 9 × 21 × 17¾ inches.

4. Connecticut Valley Tavern Parlor, c. 1750

Taverns played an important role in Colonial communities, serving as meeting places for the local citizenry and travelers. Here the townsfolk gathered to argue politics and transact business, as well as to quench their thirst. Adjacent to the taproom (visible through the door at the right) was the parlor, usually furnished with plain, sturdy pieces of the kind shown in this interior. Mrs. Thorne drew her inspiration for the chief architectural elements of this room from two historic houses in the Connecticut Valley. The corner cupboards were modeled after ones in the Harrison house in Branford; the fireplace paneling was based on that in the Mather house (which no longer exists) at Lyme. New at the time, corner cupboards ranged from unadorned types like these to more elaborate models with tops carved in the form of a half-shell (see A-6). The curvilinear heads on the paneling are typical of the region. The rectangular fire opening built into the paneling—with or without a mantel shelf above—first appeared in the early 1700s.

Next to the fireplace is a Windsor chair. In use in England from the late 1600s, such chairs began to appear in American inventories in the 1720s and remained popular for the next century. Light and durable, they were easy to construct on a lathe and were turned out in great quantities by Colonial craftsmen in a number of variations. The chair in this room is a comb-back type with a writing arm. Its straight, turned legs identify its origin as American. In Colonial times these chairs would have been painted, often dark green. The settee is also American, copied from a painted pine original depicted in N. McClelland's *Furnishing the Colonial and Federal House*. Both the slant-top desk and the tripod candle-stand to the right of the fireplace are based on Colonial models.

The cheerful chintz curtains and braided rug are characteristic of the period. The ornaments displayed in the corner cupboards represent Stafford-shire and Rockingham pieces in American collections. The former were imported from England; Rockingham ware, characterized by a lustrous, mottled, or streaked brown glaze, was made both in England and America in the early 19th century rather than in the Colonial period. The steamer print on the wall also reflects a type dating from the 19th century.

This room measures 8 × 17 × 12¾ inches.

5. Massachusetts Drawing Room, 1768

It is a far cry from the simplicity of the preceding interior to this elegant drawing room modeled after an original in the Jeremiah Lee mansion in Marblehead. Settled by fishermen from the Channel Islands, the coastal town became a prosperous fishing and merchant community. Although the early settlers of New England had been disappointed in the rocky terrain of their new home, many, like Jeremiah Lee, found great opportunities in activities related to the sea. A shipowner and merchant, he reputedly spent some

10,000 English pounds to build his mansion in 1768, borrowing architectural ideas and elements from England. It is believed that the woodwork of his parlor, richly carved in the tradition of the English architect Sir Christopher Wren (see E-4), was inspired by A. Swan's *The British Architect or the Builder's Treasury*, first published in 1745.

When it was opened to the public, the Jeremiah Lee mansion was sparsely furnished. Thus, in arranging this interior, Mrs. Thorne chose to follow her own predilections, taking her cue from the architecture of the room and from information that Lee had imported much of the contents of his house from England. The furniture here is predominantly in the Queen Anne style. Among the most striking pieces are the tall case clock and secretary acquired by Mrs. Thorne from Arthur Punt, the famous London miniature dealer. Made of walnut burl, they are exquisitely wrought replicas of English originals. Both have functioning parts: the clock can be opened and wound, and each drawer of the secretary (which also houses a secret compartment) can be opened and closed with ivory knobs the size of pinheads. The sofa was copied from an original made around 1740 and depicted on a postcard from The Metropolitan Museum of Art. The reading stand in front of the window at the left toward the back of the room is Chippendale in style. The needlepoint

rug was copied from an English design, and the draperies are of damask.

The door to the right leads to a wallpapered hallway. The use of wallpaper became more widespread in America after the mid-18th century. Jeremiah Lee imported from England special wallpaper painted entirely in tempera. Lee's wallpaper featured panels showing figures in a pastoral landscape including ancient ruins — a type of scene that recalls the paintings and prints of the 18th-century Italian artist Giovanni

Paolo Pannini. The paper between the panels emulated plasterwork in the form of Rococo scrolls and trophies. While Americans continued to import prized wallpapers from England, France, and Holland, they also began to manufacture their own, beginning with a factory set up in 1739 by upholsterer Plunkett Fleeson in Philadelphia. Early American papers relied heavily on designs copied from Europe.

On the small table in front of the fireplace is a fine chess set carved in ivory. The two portraits on the right wall are antique miniatures.

This room measures 12⅛ × 25⅞ × 21 inches.

Mrs. Thorne based this interior on a room from the Wentworth-Gardner house in Portsmouth, considered a perfect example of an American Georgian residence. The restrained paneling of Mrs. Thorne's interior is enlivened by the fine corner cupboard, with its carved half-shell interior, and by the scenic wallpaper. While both imported and domestic wallpapers had been available in America for some time (see A-5), the type of uninterrupted scenic paper represented here did not appear in America until the second decade of the 19th century. Thought to have been inspired by the painted panoramas of cities popular at the end of the 18th century and into the 19th, scenic wallpapers of this kind depicted a variety of subjects, including city and country views and scenes from literature, mythology, and history. They were made by two French concerns, Zuber of Rixheim in the Alsace and Dufour of Paris. In the 1830s Zuber produced several papers with American themes, including views of Boston Harbor and New York, and one called "The War of Independence." These papers remained popular in America through the mid-19th century.

Most of the furniture included here is modeled after American versions of the Chippendale style (see E-8). Although the Colonial craftsmen followed English designs, they often developed regional variations in the skirts of chairs and tables, the curve of the legs, the form of the ball-and-claw foot, and in the ornamental carving. For example, while the eight-legged table in this room offers certain typical elements, this particular version of the traditional gate-leg table is unusual. The side table, precursor of later sideboards, is also in the Colonial Chippendale style; such a piece often had a marble top.

The rug is a needlepoint copy of an Oriental design; the draperies are of damask. Above the fireplace hangs a coat of arms, known as a hatchment, which was customarily hung on the front door of the house following a death in the family. The mirror over the side table is in the Rococo style of the mid-18th century. The handsome coffee urn on the pedestal was based on an original depicted in J. M. Howell's *Architectural Heritage of the Piscataqua*. The brown and white and blue and white porcelains in the corner cupboard were copied from Chinese export pieces in an American collection. The side table displays finely wrought silver miniatures.

This room measures 9¾ × 14½ × 18½ inches.

7. New Hampshire Entrance Hall, 1799

Mrs. Thorne modeled this interior on the entrance hall of the John Pierce mansion in Portsmouth, attributed to the distinguished Boston architect Charles Bulfinch, who was responsible for such Boston landmarks as the Beacon Monument, the statehouse, and the courthouse. Bulfinch was strongly influenced by the work of the Adam brothers, Robert and James (see E-10), to which he was first exposed through books and then directly in England. The version of the Adams' elegant Neoclassical style of architecture, interior decoration, and furniture that Bulfinch helped popularize in America is usually referred to as the Federal style. By the 1780s wealthy Bostonians had begun to import Adam furniture and decorative objects to furnish their splendid, newly constructed houses. Residences designed by Bulfinch were assessed at the time at around $8,000, and at least one was valued at more than three times that amount.

The Neoclassical influence is easily discerned here in the elegant composition of curved and rectangular elements and in the restrained and sophisticated treatment of the walls, with their dado, fluted pilasters, and cornice. Mrs. Thorne drew her inspiration for the banisters, newel post, and painted stair runner from the *Handbook of the Concord Antiquarian Society*. The delicate carving—particularly under the soffit of the stairs—indicates the great skill of local craftsmen who had been trained originally as shipwrights. The overall white color scheme for the woodwork and plaster walls reflects a post-Revolutionary fashion.

The unique curved settee in the Hepplewhite style (see E-9) reflects an original most likely designed by Bulfinch himself for this particular space. The settee, which is mahogany with satinwood inlays, was constructed in 1799 and remained in its original location until 1948, when descendants of the Pierce family sold it to Henry Francis du Pont. Also Hepplewhite in style are the two candlestands flanking the doorway. On the floor is a petit-point version of a 17th-century Tabriz rug. Although Oriental rugs appear in New England inventories before the mid-17th century, they were expensive and therefore rare. After the mid-18th century Americans could avail themselves of more reasonably priced European carpeting, including that from Wilton (with a pile of cut loops) and Brussels (with a pile of uncut loops). The most elegant English carpeting was handwoven at the Axminster manufactory; it came in a variety of designs, including

copies of Turkish examples. Carpets began to be produced in America during the last decade of the 18th century.

This room measures 11 × 16½ × 17 inches.

8. Massachusetts Bedroom, c. 1801

This elegant bedroom of the Federal period was inspired by one of the rooms from Oak Hill, a mansion on the outskirts of Salem in what is now known as Peabody. Its architect was Samuel McIntire, son of a Salem cabinetmaker and wood-carver and himself an accomplished craftsman. McIntire's chief patron was a wealthy merchant, Elias Hasket Derby, for whose daughter Elizabeth, the wife of Captain Nathaniel West, McIntire designed this house, as well as much of its furniture. McIntire had been greatly impressed by the architectural style of the Italian Renaissance architect Andrea Palladio (see E-7), as well as by the Neoclassical designs of Robert Adam. These influences can be seen in the quiet lines and elegant decoration of this interior, most specifically in the garlands, sheaves of wheat, and baskets of flowers that decorate the mantel, doorheads, and cornice, as well as in the furniture. The decorations were either carved or cast in composition (a mixture of resin and whiting).

The bedroom, as well as two other rooms from the Oak Hill mansion, are housed in Boston's Museum of Fine Arts, along with many pieces of furniture from the Derby and West families that formed part of the original decoration. Mrs. Thorne had many of the furnishings copied from these pieces. A number are depicted in E. J. Hipkiss's *Three McIntire Rooms,* including the bed, armchair, painted chair, chandelier, and banjo clock on the rear wall.

Also original to Oak Hill are the unique mirror and bow-front commode in the Hepplewhite style. They have been attributed to Boston cabinetmaker John Seymour, as have the bed and painted chair.

Mrs. Thorne painted the material used for the window curtains and for the canopy of the poster bed in this interior, imitating the hand-painted cotton toile popular as a drapery material at the turn of the 19th century. Apparently, Elizabeth West took a deep interest in the furnishing of her home, achieving a harmonious and appealing effect that must have struck a responsive chord in Mrs. Thorne.

This room measures 11¼ × 21½ × 23 inches.

9. Massachusetts Parlor, 1818

That the influence of Robert Adam on American architecture and interior decoration continued well into the 19th century is evident in this model, based on a parlor in what was originally a private residence located in Haverhill, Massachusetts. Known at one time as Brown's Tavern and at another as Eagle House,

it was demolished in 1911. However, much of its beautiful woodwork—including mantels, cornices, and balustrades—found its way into various collections, including that of The Metropolitan Museum of Art. For many years the parlor from the Haverhill house was displayed in the Metropolitan's American Wing. In planning this

model, Mrs. Thorne referred to photographs of the museum's installation of the room.

As in other New England settings of this period created by Mrs. Thorne, the most striking aspect of this interior is the finely detailed ornament of the cornice and mantel. This would either have been cut with gouge and drill or molded in composition (see A-8) and affixed with glue.

The furniture shows the influence of designs published in George Hepplewhite's *Cabinet-maker and Upholsterer's Guide* (see E-9) and in Thomas Sheraton's *Cabinet-maker and Upholsterer's Drawing-Book* (see E-12). The shield-back chairs and the mirror over the tambour desk at the right are derived from Hepplewhite models; the sofa and the high-back chair are Sheraton designs. The stands topped with silver candlesticks flanking the desk are forerunners of the modern floor lamp. Hanging on either side of the cabinet at the left and modeled on an American piece from the last decade of the 18th century are gilded girandoles (candle sconces with inset convex mirrors), the originals of which are at the Metropolitan Museum. To the left of the fireplace stands a pole screen with a shield that could be raised and lowered to the desired height. This device helped to protect faces from the heat of the fire. The wallpaper and drapery are similar to those shown in photographs of the Metropolitan's installation of the Haverhill parlor.

Through the window can be glimpsed a view of the town commons in winter. The door on the right leads to the entrance hall of the house, which features a particularly fine doorway.

This room measures 11⅛ × 24¾ × 16 inches.

10. Massachusetts Dining Room, 1795

It has not fallen to my lot to meet a man more skilled in the useful art of entertaining his friends than Otis," wrote John Quincy Adams of Harrison Gray Otis, owner of the three-story brick house containing the dining room that inspired this interior. It is thought to be the first of three houses designed for the prosperous lawyer by the prominent Boston architect Charles Bulfinch. Preceding the John Pierce mansion (see A-7) by some four years, the Otis dining room clearly demonstrates the degree to which Bulfinch was influenced by the Neoclassical designs of English architect-decorator Robert Adam.

The Neoclassical note is most apparent in the ornamentation of the mantel and doorheads, thrown into cameo-like relief against the woodwork and walls, which have been painted in three tones of Wedgwood green. Mrs. Thorne took some liberties in creating her adaptation of this particular interior, among them increasing the space between the windows and changing the number of panes in each window from 12 to 15.

For the most part, the furniture reflects a type fashionable when Adam was at the height of his fame in Eng-

land, some three decades before the construction of Otis's first house. Derived from Hepplewhite models are the side chairs, armchairs, and the urnstands flanking the sideboard. Made of wood, the urns actually open up to reveal an interior fitted out as a knife box, with slots built in to receive the blades of the knives being stored. First used in the early part of the 18th century, such items were initially conceived as boxes with slanting tops; the urn shape was adopted later in the century and used as a decorative element by Robert Adam.

It is believed that Otis imported much of his furniture from England. The dining table, sconces, and mirror here are modeled after Adam pieces made between 1775 and 1790. The sconces were devised by Mrs. Thorne from actual Wedgwood buttons in her collection. The china cabinet is based on an English Sheraton bookcase with ormolu grillwork dating from about 1780 to 1790. The needlework rug, in the Georgian style, was copied from an original in The Art Institute of Chicago. The fine silver pieces on the sideboard were made by London silversmiths. The portrait over the sideboard is a miniature oil painting.

Clearly, this handsome residence, now the headquarters of the Society for the Preservation of New England Antiquities, was admirably suited to entertaining Harrison Gray Otis's prominent friends. Mrs. Thorne's model conveys the sense of quiet elegance that characterizes the original.

This room measures 12 × 24 × 19 inches.

11. Rhode Island Parlor, c. 1820

Prosperity created a demand for the services of architects and fine cabinetmakers in Rhode Island and elsewhere along the Atlantic Coast. As in other regions, styles and motifs popular in England found their way into the local idiom. In this interior, based on the Waterman house in Warren, typical Adamesque motifs—garlands, bow knots, and floral swags—were incorporated into the mantel, overmantel, and doorheads. The elaborate ornamentation of the dado was characteristic of the architect who designed this house, Russell Warren of Bristol, Rhode Island. Warren was active during the first three decades of the 19th century, designing some of the finest residences and public buildings in the state. Also typical of his work is the hallway through the door on the right, with its classical entrance featuring a delicate fanlight and sidelights, and plastered walls decorated with a stenciled design.

The open armchairs, the mirror on the right wall, and the tea table in front of the fireplace are modeled after originals in the American Federal style. Several of the other pieces are based on originals executed by well-known Rhode Island cabinetmakers. The card table against the left wall reflects an original dating from around 1766, designed by John Townsend of Newport. He was also responsible for the original of the blockfront chest against the right wall and, possibly, the chairs flanking the chest. The handsome secretary in the recess of the left wall reflects a model attributed to John Goddard, who established a reputation in the 1770s for his desks, secretaries, and bonnet-topped high chests of drawers. The rug is a needlepoint copy of an Oriental design. The tea service on the table is made of silver. The portrait over the fireplace is an antique miniature.

This room measures 10⅛ × 18¼ × 17½ inches.

12. Cape Cod Living Room, 1750–1850

As a contrast to the interiors of houses of wealthy merchants and prominent lawyers designed by important architects, Mrs. Thorne decided to create a more modest interior reflecting the style of life of the seafaring families of Cape Cod. Lacking the wealth of their counterparts in the bustling commercial ports of New England, the people of Cape Cod built their houses on a different scale. Efficient and well-proportioned,

with cleanly crafted interiors, Cape Cod cottages retained their essential character over the centuries, much like the weavers' cottages of England's Cotswold district.

Mrs. Thorne conceived of this room as "a typical example of a one-story cottage, small and [as] compactly planned as the boats built by the same craftsmen." The nautical touch is certainly evident in the "companionway" stairway entry and the paneling of the chimney wall. Mrs. Thorne used a monograph series published in *Pencil Points* as her reference source, modeling the rear wall on one from the MacKenzie house of Gloucester, Massachusetts, built in 1760, and the stairway after one in a house called "The Cove," in Annisquam in the same state.

The scale of the furnishings contributes to the cosy feeling of the room. Under the window stands a reproduction of what was known as a butterfly table, with drop leaves on solid swinging supports pivoted on the stretchers that join the legs. The hoop-back Windsor chairs reflect American-made models. The wing rocker is fashioned after one illustrated in S. Chamberlain's *Beyond New England Thresholds*. Also used in Europe, rockers were especially popular in America. The secretary is a modified version of an original dating from about 1700 from the Norwood house in Rockport, Massachusetts. The portrait over the secretary is an antique miniature that was once part of Mrs. Thorne's jewelry collection.

The rugs scattered on the floor, the wallpapers, and the carefully chosen prints and ornaments add a sense of warmth and intimacy, as do the child's chair and stool carrying a tiny tea set imitating the adult service on the table by the window. The tray on which the set sits was made by adding a rim to a copper penny. Mrs. Thorne was particularly proud of the minuscule bottle enclosing a clipper ship which graces the mantel shelf. Through the door we catch a glimpse of hollyhocks and a neighboring house. The window offers a view of the sea.

This room measures 7¾ × 14⅞ × 12⅛ inches.

13. New England Bedroom, 1750–1850

Like the preceding interior, this model represents a type rather than a specific room—a New England bedroom less grand than one that might have been found in the residence of a rich merchant but furnished more substantially than a bedroom in a fisherman's cottage. The lack of speci-

ficity and the long time span suggested in the dates gave Mrs. Thorne considerable latitude in her choice of decoration and furnishing styles. A variety of sources, including S. Chamberlain's *Beyond New England Thresholds,* E. Miller, Jr.'s *American Antique Furniture,* and J. Waring's *Early American Stencils,* provided Mrs. Thorne with models to imitate.

The simple partition paneling of the fireplace wall and the broad floor boards are in the style of the second half of the 18th century. Probably from a somewhat later period—perhaps the first quarter of the 19th century—is the striking stencil decoration of the plaster walls. It is modeled after an original pattern found perfectly preserved on the wall surface of an old cupboard in the Abner Goodale house in Marlborough, Massachusetts. Such patterns were traditional and were executed by itinerant stencil artists.

The handsome tester bed with its canopy, the curtains, and the high chest of drawers were inspired by examples depicted in the *Handbook of the Concord Antiquarian Society.* Both this chest and the low chest serving as a dressing table reflect mid-18th century types, while the upholstered chair was modeled after an original dated 1778 in the Abner Goodale house. All three pieces, then, would have been considered old-fashioned during most of the period covered by this room. But this was not unusual. Recent research suggests that it was customary to move out-of-date furniture from the public rooms to the bedrooms. In this interior the early pieces have been supplemented by reproductions of a Boston rocker and sewing table (to the left of the fireplace), which were not commonly used until the 1840s. The washstand with basin and ewer represented in the far left corner was standard equipment in bedrooms.

The bedspread and canopy were the work of Mrs. Thorne, who was skilled at needlework. The mantel ornaments, vases of flowers, and embroidery in progress on the stand to the left of the upholstered chair give a sense of life to this interior.

This room measures 8¼ × 19¼ × 19 inches.

14. Pennsylvania Drawing Room, 1834–36

Two yellow parlors at Andalusia, in Bensalem Township near Philadelphia, remodeled at the height of the Greek Revival period by its owner, Nicholas Biddle, inspired this drawing room. Biddle, a leading social, financial, and cultural figure in Philadelphia, was president of the Bank of the United States. As a young man, he had traveled in England, France, Italy, Greece, and elsewhere in Europe and returned to the United States convinced that the appropriate architectural idiom for the new republic was one based on classical Greek examples. These sentiments were shared by architect Benjamin Henry Latrobe, who came to the United States from England in 1796 and who, over the next 25 years, was responsible for some of the country's outstanding Greek Revival buildings. Latrobe initially had prepared designs for alterations to Andalusia, but it was another architect, Thomas U. Walter, who renovated the mansion, adding a gigantic colonnaded portico to the Delaware River side of the 18th-century farmhouse. (Both Latrobe and Walter worked independently on reconstructions and extensions of the Capitol in Washington.)

The widespread popularity in the United States of Greek architecture stemmed from the identification of American civic and political ideals with those of ancient Greece. Hoping for a time, as Latrobe put it, when "the days of Greece [would] be revived in the woods of America," Americans erected buildings of nearly every description whose forms and decoration reflected Greek prototypes.

The Greek Revival elements in this model are readily identifiable in the treatment of the ceiling, mantel, window, and doorways. Also based on classical examples are the lyre-back chairs, copied from pieces in the style of Duncan Phyfe, one of America's most celebrated furniture makers. Born in Scotland, Phyfe had come to America as a young man. He was first employed in New York as a joiner and then as a cabinetmaker, eventually becoming proprietor of a highly prosperous establishment comprising a workshop, warehouse, and showroom. Influenced by Thomas Sheraton's design books as well as by Directorate and French Empire styles (see E-25 and 26), Phyfe liked to work in mahogany, creating elegant Regency designs distinguished by the fine carving of such classical motifs as lyres, acanthus or oak leaves, and drapery swags. The armchairs flanking the game table in the center of the room were also inspired by Phyfe originals, as were the side tables seen on either side of the bookcase. Both the sofa and the armchair adjacent to it reflect American Federal-style pieces that date from between 1790 and 1800. Mrs. Thorne copied the striking girandoles over the side tables from early 19th-century ones in the collections of The Metropolitan Museum of Art, although she omitted the crystal chimneys of the originals.

While the furnishings of this interior are not reproductions of those at Anda-

lusia, they are in the same vein, for it is known that during the alterations of the mid-1830s the Biddles acquired much new furniture in the French Empire style. The total bill for the remodeling came to $14,660, far more, it is said, than Mrs. Biddle thought proper.

This room measures 13¼ × 23¾ × 20¼ inches.

15. New York City Parlor, 1850–70

Mrs. Thorne modeled this room after an interior in a reconstructed New York townhouse. The original residence was the brownstone row house at 28 East 20th Street in which Theodore Roosevelt, who became the 26th president of the United States, spent the first 14 years of his life. Razed in 1916, the house was reconstructed on its initial site in 1920 through the efforts of architect Theodate Pope Riddle, who based her work on family records, photographs, and reminiscences, as well as on measurements from an identical house. Established as a museum, the house was acquired by the National Park Service in 1963.

As was often the case, Mrs. Thorne was less concerned with creating a replica than with conveying the general appearance and tone of the interiors that inspired her models. In this instance the architectural features that reflect the townhouse include the cornice and mantel and such accessories as the wallpaper, curtains, and carpeting. The furniture is, for the most part, in the Rococo Revival style which originated in France in the 1830s in reaction to the Neoclassicism of the Revolutionary and Napoleonic periods and which spread subsequently to the Continent, England, and the United States. Rococo Revival furniture was admired for

its elaborateness and grace and remained in vogue in the United States from the 1840s until the 1870s, impinging on and eventually eclipsing the popularity of the classic designs of Duncan Phyfe (see A-14).

Among the best-known exponents of the Rococo Revival in America was John Henry Belter, a German-born cabinetmaker who immigrated to the United States in 1844 and opened a shop on Broadway in New York. Highly successful, Belter eventually established a factory on Third Avenue, where he produced elaborately carved rosewood furniture of the type used in this parlor. Characteristic of Belter's style are the rosewood sofa and armchairs, with their full upholstery, curving lines, and high, intricately pierced carved crests. To strengthen rosewood so that it would not be damaged during the carving stage, Belter invented a laminating process whereby he joined together layers of wood between slices of rosewood veneer. The resulting panels could be formed into different shapes with the use of steam heat and then carved. This method enabled him to make the one-piece molded backs that distinguish his parlor furniture. The consoles, with their marble tops, and the cabinet were also inspired by Belter originals.

The cloisonné vases on the consoles on either side of the doorway leading to

the entrance hall are antiques. The red leather book on the marble-top table to the left of the fireplace contains Abraham Lincoln's Gettysburg Address.

This room measures 12⅜ × 17½ × 21 inches.

16. Pennsylvania Drawing Room, 1761

With this interior we move back 100 years from the preceding model to pre-Revolutionary Philadelphia. The chief inspiration for this room was the State Chamber of Mount Pleasant, an ambitious Palladian structure completed in 1761 for Captain John MacPherson, a Scottish privateer. Described by John Adams as "the most elegant seat in Pennsylvania," it was owned for a time by Benedict Arnold, who would be convicted for treason during the Revolutionary War before he could occupy the house. At the time that Mount Pleasant was being planned, the standard of elegance that prevailed in Georgian England also set the tone for the wealthy residents of the Colonies. Despite the austerity of its Quaker population, Philadelphia boasted numerous splendid mansions decorated luxuriously by the finest craftsmen, many of whom had been trained in England before immigrating to America. Mount Pleasant is now operated by the Philadelphia Museum of Art and, along with other Colonial structures in Philadelphia's Fairmount Park district, is open to the public.

The rear wall of this interior, with its handsome mantel and side cupboards, is similar to the original. But instead of repeating here the residence's plain ceiling, Mrs. Thorne incorporated the Rococo design of the ceiling from the restored front room of the Powel house, installed in the Philadelphia Museum of Art. Executed by James Crowe in 1770, it illustrates the high level of plasterwork achieved in Philadelphia at this time.

Mrs. Thorne furnished this interior with pieces that are, for the most part, in a style that was known as "Philadelphia Chippendale," because of the strong influence on the city's craftsmen of Thomas Chippendale's book *The Gentleman & Cabinet Maker's Director* (see E-8). The original of the easy chair (or wing chair, as it is called today) standing to the right of the fireplace has been attributed to Benjamin Randolph who, along with William Savery and Jonathan Gostelowe, helped establish the fine reputation of Philadelphia cabinetmakers. Working in walnut and mahogany, these craftsmen became especially celebrated for their skill as carvers.

The door to the left leads to an anteroom furnished with a clock based on several created by David Rittenhouse, who made the clockworks and commissioned the cases from Philadelphia cabinetmakers.

This room measures 12 × 17½ × 18⅞ inches.

17. Pennsylvania Kitchen, 1752

Although it dates from roughly the same period as the preceding interior, this model suggests an entirely different kind of life. For this room Mrs. Thorne drew upon elements from two interiors—originally part of the Jerg Muler house in the town of Millbach—that are installed in the Philadelphia Museum of Art. Muler was the town's miller and appears to have enjoyed a comfortable standard of living. The house was typical of ones built by the Pennsylvania Dutch (more properly, Germans from the Rhineland who had originally immigrated to America in the early 18th century and who often were members of the Mennonite, Amish, Moravian, or Dunker sects). In the 20th century the Pennsylvania Dutch have come to be associated with the boldly colored, cheerful motifs—flowers, hearts, trees of life, birds, and circular discs and stars—

painted on their houses, barns, and furniture. Some of these motifs decorate the barns that form part of the scenery visible through the door at the right.

Among the most striking features of this interior is the mantel beam, scaled to represent an original that would have been almost ten feet long and hewn from a single piece of wood. The handsome corner staircase is very different in its placement and design from its counterpart in a similar New Eng-

land cottage (see A-12). Also distinctive in character are the door to the left of the staircase, with its raised and carved panels and wrought-iron hinges of regional design, and the door to the right (still known as a Dutch door), whose top portion can be opened independently of the lower part.

In general, Pennsylvania Dutch furnishings tended to resemble other country furniture of the period, although their decoration was usually distinctive. Made of oak, pine, poplar, or tulipwood, the pieces often were painted green or brown and embellished with brightly colored designs like the animals and stylized flowers that decorate the dower chest at the left, which bears the date 1797. The shelves of the two sturdy country-style dressers display pewter, brass, and pottery modeled after the highly glazed ware in green and red tones produced in Pennsylvania. The gleaming kitchen utensils and implements included around the fireplace reflect originals that would have been made in the village forge. The decorated glass standing on the center table was copied from an original by Heinrich Steigel, a German immigrant who settled in Lancaster County and became known for his glassware painted with flowers or birds or engraved after the fashion of his homeland; indeed, his pieces are barely distinguishable from ones executed in Germany.

The room measures $9\frac{1}{2} \times 24\frac{1}{8} \times 19\frac{1}{4}$ inches.

18. Shaker Living Room, c. 1800

With this interior, Mrs. Thorne moved into the special world of the utopian sect commonly called Shakers, because of the body movements its members engaged in as part of their worship. Founded in England by Quaker Ann Lee, the sect immigrated to the United States in 1774, settling first in Watervliet and New Lebanon, New York, and later establishing communities in New England, Ohio, Indiana, and Kentucky. Leading a highly regulated existence in

which equal status was accorded to women and men but celibacy and separatism were imposed in the conduct of daily life, the Shakers numbered more than 6,000 at their peak around the middle of the 19th century. Striving for self-sufficiency, their communities developed innovative agricultural and crafts techniques, first to meet their own needs and, after the mid-19th century, to respond to outside demands, as well. Several Shaker communities are now museums open to the public.

In establishing guidelines for Shaker craftsmanship, Joseph Meacham, Ann Lee's successor as head of the sect, enjoined that "all things be made . . . according to their order and use," and "be faithfully and well done, but plain and without superfluity." These qualities are, indeed, the hallmarks of the originals of the furniture included in this interior by Mrs. Thorne, who gleaned most of her models from illustrations in *Shaker Furniture* by E. D. and F. Andrews.

Mrs. Thorne's Shaker interior includes a communal living room, a study through the door at the right, and a bedroom at the left. While the main room gives the sense of order and harmony typical of a Shaker environment, the Shakers actually furnished their rooms far more sparsely and included many more built-in elements. Resembling 18th-century English country furniture, Shaker furniture is distinguished by its fine materials, flawless workmanship, and utilitarian design. A typical piece is the side chair next to the settee, with its turned back posts topped by egg-shaped finials and slat back. Perhaps best known of all are Shaker rocking chairs, an example of which can be seen to the right of the central doorway. Also typical is the secretary—commonly built into the wall—with its clean, geometric lines and turned wooden knobs. Such pieces were constructed of pine, maple, or ash with a natural finish or, in later years, stained red, yellow, blue, or green. The simplicity and efficiency of Shaker furniture, made by dedicated craftsmen

who considered the work of their hands part of their service to God, have exerted particular impact on modern American furniture design.

Mrs. Thorne was very proud of the 134 miniature objects she assembled in this interior and its side rooms—more than in any other model.

This room measures 9 × 21¾ × 24⅝ inches.

19. Maryland Dining Room, 1770–74

This interior follows rather closely the original dining room of the Hammond-Harwood house, Annapolis, built for Mathias Hammond, planter, lawyer, and later legislator, by William Buckland. The British-born master builder and architect first acquired a reputation for his work in Virginia (see A-20). Sadly, the prospective bride for whom Hammond had the house constructed turned him down, and he left Annapolis soon thereafter and became a recluse. Several generations later, the house became the property of William Harwood, great-grandson of the architect; it remained in the family until the death in 1924 of the last survivor, Harwood's daughter Hester Ann. For some years the property of St. John's College, Annapolis, the house finally came under the care of the Hammond-Harwood Association, Inc., which was formed to maintain it. The house is now open to the public.

The dining room at Hammond-Harwood is the largest room on the ground floor. A comparison of the actual interior and the model yields a very similar overall impression, despite differences in detail. The original room is notable both for its grand scale and beautifully wrought wood and plaster ornaments in the Palladian style—elements that were fashionable in England in the mid-1750s when Buckland immigrated to the Colonies. Mrs. Thorne imitated these features in the elaborately carved chimney breastwork, in the door and window heads, in the cornice, and in the coffered paneling of the shutters.

To create a sense of the furnishings of such a house as Hammond-Harwood, Mrs. Thorne copied examples in museum collections of Maryland Federal furniture dating from the 1790s. In general, the pieces reflect Sheraton models of the last decade of the 18th century, although the two side tables flanking the fireplace are models of Hepplewhite examples dating from

between 1785 and 1790. Regional in form and probably reflecting a piece made in Baltimore about 1800 is the mixing table between the two doors. The sideboard and side tables also exhibit elements of Maryland Federal furniture. Flanking the silver serving dishes on the sideboard are two knife boxes in the shape of urns, a form made popular in England by Robert Adam (see A-10). The wine cooler to the left of the sideboard opens to reveal metal compartments for storage and cooling.

This room measures 14 × 27¼ × 19 inches.

20. Virginia Dining Room, 1758

Some 16 years before he designed the house from which the preceding interior was derived, William Buckland served as architect for Gunston Hall in Fairfax County, commissioned by George Mason. Buckland had first come to the Colonies under a contract of indenture to Mason's brother; his success in Virginia led to the commissions in Maryland. The author of important resolutions voicing the Colonies' opposition to the imposition of taxes by the British and a co-author of the Constitution, Mason named his house after an ancestral home in Staffordshire, England.

In 1866 the house passed from the Mason family to a succession of occupants. The last private owners, Mr. and Mrs. Louis Hertle, undertook various improvements and renovations before deeding the house to the Commonwealth of Virginia. In her model Mrs. Thorne included several of the decorative elements introduced by them, such as the pagoda roofs over the closet doors and the large overmantel, although these have since been removed from the actual dining room. Nonetheless, the symmetry and decoration of the model strongly resemble those of the original. Gunston Hall's dining room was the first in the Colonies to be decorated in what was known as "the Chinese taste."

Since there is no record of the original furnishings, Mrs. Thorne used adaptations of Chippendale pieces, including examples in the Chinese manner depicted in various publications. In Chinese Chippendale furniture the cabriole leg is replaced by a straight leg of rectangular or clustered section, as in the pieces shown here. Also characteristic of the style is the use of fretwork as seen on the apron of the serving table against the left wall and along the base of the sideboard at the right. The center table copies one from the late 18th century. The sideboard, displaying a pair of knife cases, candlesticks, and a covered tureen, is topped by an elaborate mirror modeled after a Chippendale design. The room features many silver objects—the bases of the basket on the table and of the tureen on the sideboard are made of silver Liberty dimes, and the wine coolers on the serving table are made of 19th-century French centime pieces.

The original dining room did not include the Chinese wallpaper; the walls were plastered white, the woodwork (including the cornice, dado chair rail, and door- and window-sash trim) was painted yellow, and the baseboards dark brown.

This room measures 13¼ × 19¾ × 21⅛ inches.

This interior was inspired by the west parlor of Mount Vernon, George Washington's home for most of his adult life. Overlooking the Potomac River, the Fairfax County property had been in Washington's family for some 83 years when he inherited it in 1761. He quickly began to make improvements, redoubling his efforts after his marriage, soon thereafter, to Martha Dandridge Custis, a wealthy widow. Further additions and alterations to the house and grounds contributed to the style and comfort of the estate, as did the importation of fine furniture, rugs, and china from England. Later, Washington complained that "[these purchases] swallowed before I knew where I was all the money I got by marriage . . . nay more, brought me into debt." In 1858, when maintenance of Mount Vernon proved too burdensome for Washington's descendants and both the state of Virginia and the federal government declined to assume responsibility for the property, the Mount Vernon Ladies' Association was formed to preserve "the estate, properties and relics . . . and to open the same to the inspection of all who love the cause of liberty and revere the name of Washington."

Mrs. Thorne's interior imitates the appearance of the parlor during Washington's later years. The mantel and overmantel—with the family arms mounted between the scrolls of the pediment—are mid-18th century in style. The doorway's classical elements reveal a Palladian influence. The settee reflects a model dating from 1790 depicted in W. Nutting's *Furniture Treasury.* The high-back armchair by the fireplace, known at that time as a lolling chair and later as a Martha Washington chair, also has the tapered, straight legs typical of the American Federal period.

The Pembroke table set for tea appears to have been modeled after an original in The Metropolitan Museum of Art, and the piano after one in the collections of the Antiquarian Society of Concord, Massachusetts. The base of the music stand was derived from that of a pole screen, and the mirror was copied from a fine Federal example dating from between 1790 and 1800. The rug is a reproduction of a carpet presented to Washington which had been made at the French Aubusson manufactory. The silver tea tray is a copy of one of Martha Washington's most prized possessions. The tea set on the tray is meant to represent Chinese export ware, which was popular at the

time. A Haydn quartet rests on the music stand. The portrait in the room at the rear is a reproduction of Gilbert Stuart's *Washington at Dorchester Heights,* in the Museum of Fine Arts, Boston.

The window affords a view of the red-brick exterior of Mount Vernon.

This room measures 11⅜ × 17⅛ × 18⅝ inches.

22. Virginia Dining Room, c. 1752

In 1752 Colonel Fielding Lewis married George Washington's sister Betty and brought his wife to Kenmore, the house he had built for her in Fredericksburg on an 836-acre tract that had been surveyed by his brother-in-law. The exterior of the Georgian brick house, with its white trim, resembles that of other houses of the period, but its interior is distinctive because of the remarkable plasterwork, especially on the ceilings. Because the standard ceiling height at the time was 14 feet and the Kenmore ceilings are 12½ feet, it is thought that the plasterwork may have been added later. Documents found at Mount Vernon refer to a Frenchman as having executed the plasterwork; in two rooms the ceiling patterns were derived from B. Langley's *The City and Country Builder's and Workman's Treasury of Designs,* first published in London in 1740 and reissued in subsequent years.

As indicated in "Creating the Thorne Rooms" (see pages 21-23), Mrs. Thorne took some liberties with this interior, moving the doors away from the flanking walls toward the fireplace and substituting the elaborate mantel and overmantel from another room at Kenmore for the simpler paneling that comprises the overmantel in the actual dining room. The furniture now at Kenmore is not original to the estate, since the house passed out of the family after Betty Lewis died in 1797 and its contents were dispersed. The house suffered considerable damage in later years, especially during the Civil War. In 1922, when it was in danger of being destroyed, it was acquired by the Fredericksburg chapter of the National Society of the Daughters of the American Revolution and eventually was refurnished with the help of Louise du Pont Crowninshield, working together with museum curators. Mrs. Thorne created a similar ambience, but with pieces copied from a variety of sources.

Although Mrs. Thorne described this interior as being from the mid-18th century, the furnishings, such as the sideboard, window seat, and mirror, are actually modeled after American Federal examples dating for the most part from the 1790s. Mrs. Thorne modified the mirror by adding chains from the eagle to the urns. The dining room table represents a type of the last quarter of the 18th century, and the commodes reflect originals that date from 1800. The silver compotes on the sideboard at the left are from Tiffany's and bear the mark of the noted silversmith John C. Moore.

The windows open onto a broad portico with white columns. Across a garden can be glimpsed a portion of the exterior of Kenmore, to allow the viewer to visualize the mansion over which Betty Washington Lewis presided.

This room measures 14 × 21 × 21¼ inches.

23. Virginia Drawing Room, 1754

Another Virginia interior from the mid-18th century, this model was inspired by the drawing room of Wilton, a ten-room Georgian house known today for its outstanding brickwork and built by William Randolph III along the James River south of Richmond. Although its architect is unknown, the house has been attributed to Richard Taliaferro, designer of the George Wythe house in Williamsburg, which it strongly resembles. Frequented by such distinguished guests as George Washington, the Marquis de Lafayette, and Thomas Jefferson (a Randolph on his mother's side), Wilton survived the Civil War and a succession of owners relatively intact. In 1923, however, its site threatened by industrial encroachment, the house was in danger of being dismantled. It was saved by the Virginia chapter of the National Society of the Colonial Dames of America, which purchased it and removed it to another location six miles upriver. Reconstructed and refurnished with the help of family inventories, Wilton is now open to the public; the society uses the basement as its headquarters.

Wilton is notable particularly for the paneling that graces every room and for its handsome cornices with their dentil moldings. Although Mrs. Thorne omitted this latter detail, she reproduced here the chief architectural features of the back wall of the original drawing room, including the fluted pilasters of the fireplace and flanking arches. At Wilton, however, alcoves intervene between the archways and the windows. The marble mantel of the model imitates the original, which was English in style. The elaborate plasterwork of the ceiling in Mrs. Thorne's interior reflects a later style.

The furniture reproduced by Mrs. Thorne here is primarily in the Queen Anne style, which remained in vogue in the Colonies until after the mid-18th century. The most striking pieces are the "japanned" high chest of drawers along the left wall and the low chest of drawers to the left of the doorway, inspired by American examples of the

1730s and 1740s. "Japanning" was a method of imitating Oriental lacquering which involved the application to wood of many layers of a compound of seedlac or shellac dissolved in spirits of wine and most often colored black, red, or dark green. The decorations were outlined in gold size, built up, then colored and gilded. Mrs. Thorne added a number of intimate touches to this room, including the tea table set with a service, and a delicate bird cage complete with three canaries. As a whole, the interior conveys a sense of the elegance and comfort enjoyed by the owners of the James River plantations of Virginia.

This room measures 12 × 19⅝ × 22 inches.

The original of this magnificent hall is to be found in Carter's Grove, a plantation house located on a bluff eighty feet above the James River, some six miles southeast of Williamsburg. Its original owner, Carter Burwell, was the grandson of Robert "King" Carter, so called because of his vast holdings — 300,000 acres of land and 1,000 slaves — and influence. Built over a period of years, the main house was completed in 1755 by masons and carpenters from the Williamsburg area. The fine woodcarving, however, was supervised by an Englishman, Richard Baylis, brought over from England for that purpose. Burwell did not enjoy for long what was commonly agreed to be one of the finest houses in Virginia; he died within a year of its completion. The house remained in the family until 1838, after which it had a succession of owners until it was purchased in 1928 by Mr. and Mrs. Archibald M. McCrea, who renovated and enlarged the house extensively. It is now owned and operated by the Colonial Williamsburg Foundation.

The woodwork throughout Carter's Grove took some three years to execute and is one of its most striking features. In this entrance hall the original paneling, long covered with layers of paint, was found to be native walnut and pine. The stairway, with its beautifully carved railing, is considered one of the finest of its period. It still bears the scars said to have been inflicted on it by the sabers of enemy dragoons, who slashed the handrails as they rode their horses up and down the staircase when the British occupied the house during the Revolutionary War.

Mrs. Thorne furnished the hall with copies of Philadelphia furniture whose style falls between the earlier and simpler Queen Anne mode and the later, more elaborate Rococo-inspired forms published by Thomas Chippendale (see E-8). Until recently, historians assumed, as Mrs. Thorne probably did, that the good pieces of furniture in Colonial Virginia had been imported from England or the North. However, a recent exhibition featuring the work of Colonial cabinetmakers from Williamsburg and the surrounding area demonstrated the high degree of skill shown by Virginia craftsmen. Thus, it is possible that the owners of the James River plantations might well have had

some of their fine furniture made locally.

This room measures 14 × 18¼ × 22 inches.

25. Virginia Drawing Room, 1755

This model, like the preceding one, is also based on an interior from Carter's Grove, in this case, the southeast drawing room. Once again, the most striking feature is the finely executed paneling which in the original was made of native walnut and pine. Especially noteworthy is the treatment of the fireplace wall, which combines the raised paneling used throughout the room with a white marble mantel framed by stately pilasters. The cornice is denticulated.

Mrs. Thorne furnished this interior with reproductions of both English and American Chippendale designs, depicted in the reference works she used most frequently. The desk, for example, is adapted from a piece dating from about 1740 illustrated in P. Macquoid's *Dictionary of English Furniture,* although Mrs. Thorne omitted the paw feet and changed the side paneling. The Chippendale corner chair next to the desk reflects a model produced in America between 1755 and 1785. The two chests flanking the door on the left wall are swell-front New England designs dating from around 1780. The tea table next to the fireplace at the left combines elements from several Colo-

nial designs. In front of the door in the right corner stands an embroidery frame with a piece of partially completed work. The chandelier is copied from one in The Metropolitan Museum of Art. The "bull's eye" mirror over the mantel is in the Empire style of a much later period.

With its fine paneling, stately furniture, and decorative porcelains, this interior attempts to convey the comfortable elegance of the original drawing room in Carter's Grove. Carter Burwell had been reared in the Colonial equivalent of an aristocratic tradition, and when he planned his house he chose the best models available. Richard Baylis, who came with his family from England to supervise the three-year-long task of paneling the house by the James River, justified his employer's faith in every way. More than 200 years after it was built, the interior of Carter's Grove continues to evoke the admiration of its many visitors.

This room measures 13¾ × 20¼ × 18¼ inches.

26. Virginia Dining Room, c. 1800

Mrs. Thorne designated this interior as "Jeffersonian," although she was careful not to represent it as a model of the dining room at Monticello in Charlottesville, Virginia, Thomas Jefferson's residence from his 20s until the end of his life. Jefferson began to build Monticello in 1772, bringing his young wife Martha there before it was completed. In the course of the next eight years he became a delegate to the Continental Congress, governor of Virginia, minister to France, secretary of state, vice president, and, in 1800, third president of the United States.

A man of extraordinarily wide interests, Jefferson mastered many disciplines, including horticulture, music, and architecture. His love of classical architecture was intensified during the five years he spent as American minister in France. "From Lyons to Nîmes," he wrote, "I have been nourished with the remains of Roman grandeur." Seeking to "improve the taste of my countrymen, to increase their reputation . . . and procure them . . . praise," he designed the new capitol of Virginia after the "Maison Carrée," the Roman temple at Nîmes. He also designed the University of Virginia (which he founded) according to classical architectural principles. Monticello also benefited from his time abroad, which inspired Jefferson to add the famous octagonal dome and outward-facing portico.

It was her desire to portray Jefferson's skill as an architect and innovator that led Mrs. Thorne to include in this interior several features from Monticello that have been attributed to his ingenuity. The side doors of the actual mantel communicate directly with the wine cellar. The three sections of the window along the left wall reflect an invention by Jefferson to facilitate control of ventilation. He is also credited with the folding doors at the rear that lead to a representation of the celebrated "tea room" extension, which houses the "busts in plaister" of four figures revered by Jefferson— George Washington, the Marquis de Lafayette, Benjamin Franklin, and John Paul Jones—executed by the French sculptor Jean Antoine Houdon.

Although the original furnishings of Monticello have long been dispersed, Mrs. Thorne decorated this room with copies of originals in the Empire style from the first two decades of the 19th century. The banquet table is a replica of Jefferson's own table, while the chairs and side tables copy pieces in the style of Duncan Phyfe dating from between 1800 and 1820. The crystal chandelier and brackets are modeled after ones at The Metropolitan Museum of Art, and the crystal pieces on the table replicate originals in the collections of The Art Institute of Chicago. The needlepoint rug follows an Empire pattern of French origin.

Jefferson, who died in 1826, spent the last 17 years of his life at Monticello. "My mornings are devoted to correspondence," he wrote. "From breakfast to dinner, I am in my shops, my garden, or on horseback among my farms; from dinner to dark I give to society and friends; and from candle light to early bed-time, I read."

This room measures 13 × 22½ × 14½ inches.

27. Virginia Kitchen, 18th Century

Mrs. Thorne modeled this interior after the kitchen of the reconstructed Governor's Palace complex in Williamsburg. First settled in 1633 and later named capital first of the colony and then of the Commonwealth of Virginia, Williamsburg lost its central role after Richmond became the capital in 1780. Among the most important buildings in the town was the Governor's Palace, constructed between 1708 and 1720, which served as the residence of seven royal governors and the first two Commonwealth governors, Patrick Henry and Thomas Jefferson (see A-26). After the removal of the capital to Richmond, the palace served as a military hospital until it was destroyed by fire in 1781.

In 1931, some five years after John D. Rockefeller, Jr. had embarked on the restoration of Colonial Williamsburg, work was begun on the reconstruction of the Governor's Palace on its original site. Based on archeological and documentary evidence, including a plan of the first floor drawn by Jefferson, the reconstructed palace was completed in 1934, though additional research and new information have led to continuing modifications. A critical source for the re-creation of the interior as it would have been in the 1770s was the inventory of furnishings and personal belongings taken after the death of British governor Norborne Berkeley, the Baron de Botetourt.

The kitchen of the Governor's Palace was located in one of the outlying structures, close to the scullery, smokehouse, salthouse, wine cellar, and kitchen garden. Easily accessible was a canal, which in the summer was stocked with fish and in winter became a source of ice. An orchard also was close at hand.

Since much of the menial work was done in the scullery, the kitchen itself, as reflected in Mrs. Thorne's interior, was relatively free of clutter. The cooking was done in the great central fireplace, with its hanging crane and dutch oven used for baking in front of an open fire. The kinds of metal cooking utensils hanging on the mantel would have been made locally. Illustrated articles on the Williamsburg restoration became the source for many of the pieces in Mrs. Thorne's model, including the cupboard, table, Windsor chairs, ladder-back chair against the left wall, banister-back chair to the left of the dresser and high chair to the right, and closed cupboard at the foot of the stairs. The stairs would have led to a storeroom. A butter churn stands to the right of the door, which opens onto a kitchen garden. Through the window at the right can be seen an iron pot in which soft soap would have been made over an outside fire.

Since the kitchen was at some distance from the formal dining room in the main house, the food was carried to the table in covered dishes. This would have been no small task on occasions such as the following, described by the Baron de Botetourt in a letter of 1769: "Fifty-two dined with me yesterday

and I expect at least that number today."

This room measures 10 × 20 × 20½ inches.

28. South Carolina Drawing Room, 1775–1800

Founded by English settlers, Charleston has occupied since 1680 its present site at the head of the bay formed by the confluence of the Ashley and Cooper rivers. Despite a devastating fire in 1740, the city, by the latter part of the 18th century, had become the commercial and cultural center of the South. Its population augmented by French Huguenots fleeing religious persecution in their homeland, Charleston was early on a cosmopolitan city surrounded by great plantations where rice, indigo, and cotton were grown. Many of its splendid townhouses were built and maintained by the planters who helped create the wealth of the region. Some of the finest houses date from the last quarter of the 18th and first quarter of the 19th centuries, the period Mrs. Thorne chose to represent here.

This interior is a composite of the second-floor drawing room of a house built by Colonel John Stuart in 1770 and of a considerably later addition built over the garden and used as a dining room. The mantel and doorways were derived from the earlier room, the bay window from the later one. The woodwork of both rooms is in the collection of the Minneapolis Institute of Arts. The very English character of the detail reproduced by Mrs. Thorne—especially of the doors and overmantel—reflects Charleston's cultural kinship with England and the West Indies rather than with the northern colonies on the Atlantic seaboard.

Mrs. Thorne furnished the interior with American Neoclassical pieces. The gate-leg table set for tea in front of the fireplace and the hanging shelves on either side of the bay were copied from originals depicted in P. Macquoid's *Dictionary of English Furniture*. The settee and high-back armchair are in the Hepplewhite mode. The bookcase along the right wall is a much altered version of a Sheraton sideboard; the drum table in the bay and the armchair in the foreground are also based on Sheraton designs.

The globe beside the bookcase at the right, copied from a pair of antique examples depicted in a 1939 issue of *Connoisseur* magazine, and the Chinese rugs and screen symbolize Charleston's far-flung connections.

This room measures 12¼ × 22¼ × 21½ inches.

29. South Carolina Ballroom, 1775–1835

The principal sources for this elegant interior were architectural elements from the first-floor hall and second-floor ballroom of the William Gibbes house at 64 South Battery in Charleston. A planter and merchant, Gibbes built the handsome three-story clapboarded dwelling, described as "of the purest Georgian style," in 1772. A man of wealth and culture, he had the residence designed in a combination of local and English styles. After the Revolution, the house passed to Sarah Moore Smith and remained in the same family for four generations. Around 1800 some of the rooms were remodeled in the Adam style. Descriptions of the house indicate that much of the Georgian woodwork, originally imported from England, was ornamented at this time with hard putty decoration.

One of these renovated interiors was the ballroom, which has been praised for its imported Italian stucco ceiling, wood-paneled walls, mantel, and wide-plank flooring. The Adam influence is immediately apparent in the cornice, doorway, and window surrounds of Mrs. Thorne's interior. The two monumental columns at the rear of the model, however, are actually located in the broad hall that runs the full length of the Gibbes house. Several elements of this interior, especially the Palladian-style window at the rear of the room, were inspired by another Charleston residence, the Radcliffe-King house, built in 1806.

The Gibbes house survived the Revolution, the Civil War, and an earthquake in 1886 relatively undamaged. In 1930 it was bought and extensively restored by Mrs. Washington A. Roebling, whose husband had helped build the Brooklyn Bridge.

In furnishing this interior Mrs. Thorne chose to imitate primarily American Empire pieces of the kind made fashionable by New York furniture makers. The sofa was modeled after an example from between 1810 and 1820, which is also the period when the original of the mahogany desk and bookcase along the right wall was made. Featuring stencil decorations between and on the pilasters themselves, the piece has striking ornate legs and gilded feet, as does the companion console table against the left wall. The closed armchair to the right of the console is a reproduction of one of a pair inlaid with brass, a type made popular by Duncan Phyfe. The piano is a copy of one made by John Tallman of New York in 1825. The musical instruments, the torchères in front of the columns, the ornamental urns on the mantel, and the vases of flowers enhance the impression of elegance and cultivation that Mrs. Thorne wished to convey in this interior.

This room measures 15½ × 19¾ × 30⅞ inches.

30. Georgia Double Parlor, c. 1850

The last of the 13 colonies to be founded, Georgia was settled by the British in 1733 primarily to protect the Carolinas from the Spanish. Exporting such products as lumber, rice, and indigo to England, Georgia became a thriving colony, achieving even greater prosperity when its plantations began to grow cotton, especially after the invention of the cotton gin by Eli Whitney in 1793. It is a plantation interior of the affluent

decade before the outbreak of the Civil War that Mrs. Thorne chose to suggest in this model.

The construction of some of the most splendid plantation houses coincided with the popularity of the Greek Revival style (see A-14). As an accommodation to the hot summers of the region, many plantation houses were built around a central hall running from front to back to allow for free circulation of air. Frequently, a double parlor was situated along one side of the house, the two spaces connected through an archway which, in some cases, could be closed with double doors.

In this interior Mrs. Thorne composed such a setting, endowing it with lofty ceilings, ornate cornice and mantel, and handsome archways. The furnishings are derived not only from histories of the decorative arts of the period but also from the popular conception of ante-bellum plantation interiors depicted in the sets of the film "Gone with the Wind" (1939). That dramatic rendering of Margaret Mitchell's novel did a great deal to create a visual vocabulary for the time and places it embraced. Thus, Mrs. Thorne's notes for this room include an article from the November 1939 issue of *House & Garden,* with an illustration of the bay from Aunt Pittypat's parlor, which provided the model for the bay in this interior. Another magazine article was the source of the elaborately carved "chaperone" sofa in the bay, con-

structed to prevent its occupants from sitting too close to one another. Next to the sofa is a replica of a footrest known as a gout stool. The secretary was based on a Victorian original from about 1860, and the center table on an English model depicted in an illustrated catalogue of 1851. Several pieces, including the upholstered chair to the right of the fireplace, the piano, and the piano stool were inspired by examples from homes in Natchez, Mississippi.

On the floor is a rug of the Wilton type (named after the English town in which this kind of carpeting was produced). Such carpeting, woven on Jacquard looms, usually covered the whole floor. The console with its carved legs, the assortment of small tables, the elaborate mirror, the lamps, the ornaments and objects—especially the waxed fruits and flower arrangement

under glass on the center table and the operable stereopticon on the table between the two spaces—evoke many aspects of English and American Victorian parlors (see E-14 and A-15).

The front room measures 14 × 21 × 24 inches.

31. Tennessee Entrance Hall, 1835

Mrs. Thorne modeled this interior after the hall of The Hermitage, home of Andrew Jackson, who served two terms as the seventh president of the United States, from 1829 to 1837. During his second term the original building on his 625-acre property outside Nashville was severely damaged by fire, and a new one was constructed on the foundations of the old. Hero of the expedition against the Creek Indians in 1813 and of the Battle of New Orleans against the British in 1815, Jackson as a political figure aligned himself with the common man against moneyed interests, but his own style of life was within the tradition of the Southern gentleman. The Hermitage is a Greek Revival mansion consisting of a central porticoed pavilion with flanking wings. The main portion of the residence is distinguished by handsome white columns and wide verandas outside and spacious rooms inside.

The most striking feature of Mrs. Thorne's model, and of the actual hall, is the Neoclassical spiral staircase. The wallpaper is in the mode of, though not identical to, the paper used in the original; Mrs. Thorne copied a similar paper owned by The Art Institute of Chicago. The pattern of this paper, made by the French firm of Dufour (see A-6), depicts "The French in Egypt" and dates from 1814. The furniture in the hall is of the late classical type popular in the 1830s and '40s known as pillar and scroll. The sofa is in the Empire style, the chair along the left wall in the Directorate style (see E-25). The console and table were inspired by pieces in The Hermitage.

Through the door at the left can be glimpsed a study furnished with copies of other pieces from The Hermitage, including a table and desk chair in 18th-century Chippendale style . They were made from the wood of the frigate *Constitution,* nicknamed "Old Ironsides," which earned its laurels in the 1812 war against the British. The gilt-bronze mantel clock undoubtedly replicates 19th-century French examples made for export to the United States. These included depictions of beloved figures like George Washington and Benjamin Franklin. Over the mantel hangs a portrait of Jackson. The paper stand holds a replica of an 1835 newspaper.

This room measures 14⅛ × 14½ × 30¼ inches.

32. Louisiana Bedroom, 1800–50

Claimed for France by the explorer La Salle in 1682, Louisiana became a Spanish possession in 1763, reverting briefly to France before Jefferson negotiated the Louisiana Purchase in 1803. Located on the Mississippi River, some 100 miles from the Gulf of Mexico, New Orleans became a thriving commercial center, known for its slave and cotton markets

and high living. For most of the 19th century the mixture of Franco-Spanish and local culture, known as Creole, remained the dominant influence in the city.

In the Vieux Carré, the old French Quarter, houses were often built around enclosed courtyards and festooned with cast- and wrought-iron balconies in what became a distinctive New Orleans style. Many of the city's most splendid mansions date from the 1830s and '40s, when the Greek Revival fashion was at its height. This style was modified in New Orleans by the French Empire and Georgian styles. In composing this boudoir and the bedroom to the right, Mrs. Thorne used elements from a number of houses depicted in I. W. Ricciuti's *New Orleans and Its Environs,* including the Girod house in the Vieux Carré, which inspired the mantel; the Hurst plantation on the outskirts of the city, which provided the model for the archway and window trim; and the Forsyth house in the Garden district, from which the cornice was copied.

The furniture of this interior is mainly in the Empire style, most of the pieces having been fashioned after originals made between 1820 and 1830. Most striking is the chaise longue, a fine example of what was known as a Meridienne, which Mrs. Thorne adapted from an original shown in E. Miller, Jr.'s *American Antique Furniture,* also the source of the Empire-style bureau, with its elaborately curved columns, feet, and accompanying mirror supports. The elegant dressing table

and mirror at the back wall were modeled after items in photographs in an unidentified source. This table, its chair, the pole screen, side chair in the boudoir, and small ballroom chairs in the bedroom are copied from English or French examples of inlaid and gilt papier-mâché furniture, which was popular from the 1840s through the 1870s. The side tables, with their elaborate lyre bases, were inspired by an

Empire-style sofa table. The elaborate mirrors above the tables reflect mahogany-framed examples illustrated in W. Nutting's *Furniture Treasury,* although Mrs. Thorne was responsible for the incorporation of pictures into the design and for the addition of gilt. Touches like these, as well as the spaciousness, the fine carpets, the elegant accoutrements on the dressing table,

and the objets d'art scattered on the small tables in both rooms evoke a strong sense of the French origins of New Orleans.

This room measures 13 × 19 × 19 inches.

33. "Middletown" Parlor, 1875–1900

In 1929 sociologists Robert S. and Helen M. Lynd published their study of a "typical" small city entitled *Middletown,* followed by a sequel which appeared in 1937. That their material had been gathered in Muncie in Mrs. Thorne's native Indiana suggests that her choice of name for this interior was not accidental. The setting has a certain poignance because it represents the time and place of Narcissa Niblack Thorne's own childhood. While the style of furniture and decoration shown here was not only out of fashion but in disrepute by the time Mrs. Thorne was creating this model, there is a strong sense of affectionate reminiscence in the attention to detail. As she wrote about this room, "It makes you feel as though you were visiting your grandmother."

The most striking architectural element of this interior is the bay to the left of the room, with its Gothic Reviv-

al windows. Such decorative details as the fret- and scrollwork across the top of the opening of the bay embellished the exteriors and interiors of a multitude of Midwestern homes. The hallway at the rear is decorated with period wallpaper and furnished with what was known as a hall tree, designed to hold not only hats but also umbrellas and footgear. The opening at the right leads to a substantial dining room, its table covered by a white cloth. The massive Renaissance Revival sideboard was inspired by an 1851 bookcase.

Mrs. Thorne derived most of the eclectic Revival-style furniture in the parlor from photographs and clippings, many of them from issues of *Antiques Magazine*. This was the source of the ornate Renaissance Revival secretary against the back wall. The chairs by the door to the hallway and in the right foreground were modeled after pieces that formed part of a simplified Rococo Revival parlor suite depicted in photographs published by The Art Institute of Chicago, as was that ubiquitous period piece, the spool-turned étagère or whatnot, displaying family treasures and bric-a-brac. The photograph hanging to the left of the fireplace is of Abraham Lincoln and his son Tad. Occupying the corresponding spot to the right of the mantel is a paper rack containing a copy of the *Chicago Daily Tribune*. The Renaissance Revival center table displays a photograph of Ulysses S. Grant.

The two rooms are full of reminders of the revolution wrought in American

households by the mass production of such items as wallpaper, carpeting, furniture, and household wares. An example of patent furniture is the upholstered platform rocker, in front of the hallway door, which reflects a type first introduced in the 1870s. The chief advantage of this chair was that it rocked in place, thus saving wear and tear on the carpet and walls. The steam locomotive on the floor at the right is a solid gold miniature presented to Mrs. Thorne by her friend and fellow miniatures enthusiast actress Colleen Moore, whose "Fairy Castle" is displayed at Chicago's Museum of Science and Industry. Next to this piece sits an antique jointed doll. Along the left wall, close to the doorway, hangs that harbinger of a more frantic future, the telephone, invented by Alexander Graham Bell in 1876.

This room measures 10⅛ × 21 × 18½ inches.

The unique blend of Spanish and American Indian cultures that distinguishes the Southwest and that is illustrated in this New Mexican interior was hard-won. From the 16th century on, much violence and bloodshed occurred before the Europeans came to dominate life in this dry, dramatically beautiful land. The dining room created here by Mrs. Thorne was inspired by modern New Mexican versions of the missions and haciendas constructed with European and American Indian techniques by the Spanish who settled New Mexico as ranchers, miners, and farmers during the 18th and 19th centuries.

The thick walls—made of adobe bricks laid in mud mortar, mud-plastered, and white-washed—of the interiors that served as models for Mrs. Thorne's room protected the inhabitants from the extreme heat and cold of the desert. Mud also covered the roof, supported by *vigas,* or large ceiling beams made of native pine. Between the beams can be seen *latillas,* aspen or cedar saplings arranged in a herring-bone pattern, a technique developed originally to insulate the rooms and to prevent dirt from sifting down from the mud roof. The floor was also made of earth, painted and polished. The traditional beehive or semicircular corner fireplace recalls a shape incorporated by Pueblo Indians in their structures, some of which Mrs. Thorne included in the scene outside the window.

The furniture in this room was inspired by examples used in 20th-century New Mexican homes. Made of pine, oak, and walnut, these substantial pieces, with their simple, rectangular shapes and carved and painted decorations, reflect Mexican and Spanish prototypes. The tin shrine over the sideboard, the votive figure on the mantel, and the sconces flanking the doorway are Mexican in design. Much of the silver in this room, as well as the pottery and rugs, was found in Mexico City.

Through the doorway at the right is a tiled hallway with a staircase.

This room measures 12 × 17 × 16¾ inches.

35. California Living Room, c. 1935–40

Santa Barbara's magnificent mountain and ocean views and fair climate have made it, since the late 1890s, one of America's favorite retreats from winter. In the early decades of the 20th century a signifi cant number of Santa Barbara buildings were constructed in a freely interpreted Mediterranean style that evoked the city's Spanish Colonial heritage. The greatest practitioner of the Spanish Revival style was architect George Washington Smith, who was active in the Santa Barbara area from 1916 to 1930.

Smith's popularity was due to his successful adaptation of the Spanish Colonial or Mission styles to contemporary use, incorporating flexible plans, romantic details, and arrangements sensitive to the surrounding landscape. Inspired by the string of missions established by the Spanish in California from the 16th century on, Smith combined in his interiors the Moorish and Southern European ele-

ments that characterize Spanish architecture, such as the timber-work of the
ceiling, the carved and gilded door, the
elaborately patterned tiles on and
around the staircase, and the gleaming
floor tiles in this interior.

The furniture assembled in this
room reflects the eclectic taste prevalent in the United States during the
1920s and '30s. While many of the
heavy, dark wood pieces suggest Spanish prototypes from the 15th through
the 18th centuries, the four-chair-back
settee departs from the Spanish-in-
spired idiom, as do the Oriental jars on
the chest at the left and the large modern table lamp at the right.

Undoubtedly, Mrs. Thorne was familiar with rooms like the one she
created in this model. Not only did interior design magazines of her time
feature articles about the decoration of
fashionable California resort homes,
but many of her acquaintances and
friends wintered in Santa Barbara and
nearby communities and lived in environments similar to this one.

This room measures 12¼ × 29⅞ ×
23 inches.

36. California Living Room, 1850–75

Monterey — the capital of northern California for most of the period from 1775 until 1847, when the Californios or Spanish colonists who had controlled California since the late 16th century were defeated by the United States — was a whaling and fishing center. Its prosperity led to the development of a cultural life. The site of California's first theater in 1844, the town also boasted the region's first newspaper, established in 1846.

The port city provided the setting of the Casa Soberanes, which inspired this interior by Mrs. Thorne. California's first two-story house, the Casa Soberanes was built between 1842 and 1849 by Rafael Estrada, half-brother of Governor Juan Alverado. Bought in 1860 by the Soberanes family, it was restored in the 1920s. Monterey-style houses were constructed of adobe and included a hip roof, balcony, and veranda (like the one seen through the door and win-

dows of this interior). The thick walls, inside shutters, and ceiling timbers are all elements that were common to Spanish Colonial buildings. The original earth floor of the Casa Soberanes was replaced by stained wooden planks during the house's restoration.

Although the architectural setting is Spanish Colonial, the furnishings are primarily simple American examples of the 1840s through the mid-century. The somewhat spare interior and the mixture of styles may be an indication of Mrs. Thorne's awareness of the difficulty and expense of transporting fur-

niture West from sources of manufacture in the East. The stenciled rocker was inspired by a type produced in certain sections of New England between 1825 and 1830. The two tables, with their flat, unadorned surfaces and C-scroll supports, are examples of pillar and scroll furniture popular in the 1830s and '40s. The bench in front of the fireplace imitates an American Federal design dating from the early years of the 19th century. The wooden fire-

place, with its split-spindle and turned ornament, reflects a New England type. The hooked rugs placed here were not actually in use in California at this time.

The stairs seen in the hallway beyond the door at the left would have led to the bedrooms.

This room measures 10 × 22 × 16¼ inches.

37. California Hallway, c. 1940

Decorating is eliminating," wrote American furniture designer Paul T. Frankl in his influential *New Dimensions* in 1928. "Simple lines are modern. They are restful to the eye and dignified and tend to cover up the complexity of the machine age. If they do not completely do this, they at least divert our attention and allow us to feel ourselves master of the machine." This interior, which was described by Mrs. Thorne as a "modern art gallery," seems to follow Frankl's prescription for a truly modern decor. The dark floor and off-white carpet, architectural treatment of the walls, and restrained furnishings all serve to highlight a remarkable collection of actual works of art in miniature.

To the left of the French doors is a gouache painting entitled *Au Bord de la mer (At the Seaside)* by Jean Victor Hugo (born 1894), grandson of the famous 19th-century French writer. To the right of the doors is a crayon drawing, *Promenade dans la forêt (Walk in the Forest),* by Marie Laurencin (1885–1956), who figured prominently in the circle around Pablo Picasso in Paris before World War I. Two bronze sculptures of standing female nudes by the American sculptor John Storrs (1885–1956) are placed in the curtained window recesses to either side of the fireplace. On the chimney breast hangs a still life in oil by the French Cubist painter Amédée Ozenfant (1886–1966). Over the couch at the right is a composition in gouache by the French Cubist painter Fernand Léger (1881–1955). The four watercolor compositions arranged on either side of the couch are the work of another French painter, Léopold Survage (1879–1968). Mrs. Thorne commissioned the works by Léger, Ozenfant, and Survage especially for this room.

The furniture in this San Francisco penthouse interior—with its flat surfaces, low lines, and pronounced angles—is typical of the international modernist style that came to the United States from France. Also characteristic of this style is the use of occasional bright color spots, as in the red upholstery; of modern materials like the plastic in the two chairs on either side of the couch; and of light wood veneers, as in the coffee table and one-arm benches.

Through the French doors a spectacular view of San Francisco offers a glimpse of part of Treasure Island and the then newly built Golden Gate Bridge (completed in 1937), silhouetted by twinkling lights against the night sky.

This room measures 13⅞ × 16⅝ × 19¾ inches.

Glossary of Selected Terms

Arabesque—intricate surface decoration of Near Eastern origin consisting of interlaced stylized foliage, scrolls, and flowing lines.

Armoire—a large wardrobe or cupboard decorated with architectural elements such as pilasters.

Armoire à deux corps—a type of case furniture (see below) made up of two cupboards, each with two doors and set one above the other, the upper one being narrower and recessed.

Aubusson carpet manufactory—French factory which produced smooth-faced, tapestry-woven carpets in the late 18th and early 19th centuries.

Baluster—short post, often circular in section, with a varied profile, and used in a series that supports a railing; term is also applied to similar forms incorporated into decorative objects.

Banquette—small bench, usually upholstered, seating two or three people.

Beauvais tapestry manufactory—French royal tapestry factory founded in 1664, which originally produced tapestries of foliage and landscape patterns (verdures), and later a wide variety of subjects; merged with the Gobelins manufactory (see below) in 1940.

Bergère—armchair with rounded back, wide seat, and upholstery between arm crest and seat.

Blanc-de-chine—French term for porcelain produced in the Tê-hua factories in Fukien province, China, and associated mainly with the Ch'ing dynasty (1644-1912); this lustrous, white glaze was used most notably on statuettes.

Cabinetmaker—a term used specifically to refer to a highly skilled furniture maker, especially in late 17th-century Europe, when cabinets were generally the most elaborate pieces of furniture made.

Cabriole leg—form of furniture leg that curves outward at the knee and tapers inward, terminating in a foot of various configurations; first appeared in Europe about 1700, inspired by Chinese models.

Carcass—main structure of a piece of furniture, to which veneers (see below) may be applied.

Carnelian—red variety of chalcedony (quartz), used for decorative objects and jewelry.

Case furniture—box-like furniture forms designed to contain or enclose something, e.g., chest of drawers, cupboard, etc.

Chaise longue—chair with an elongated seat accommodating a single, reclining person.

Château—French feudal castle; later, the term was applied to a large country house and estate, usually in France.

Chelsea porcelain factory—renowned English soft-paste porcelain manufactory, founded in the mid-18th century.

Chinoiserie—Western imitations or interpretations of Chinese art.

Commode—French name for a chest of drawers.

Composition—a mixture of whiting, resin, and size used from the 18th century on for molded decorations, usually affixed with glue or panel pins.

Console—side table supported by two or more legs or brackets and intended to be placed against a wall, its top usually of marble.

Cornice—any projecting horizontal, ornamental molding.

Coromandel lacquer—type of vividly colored lacquer with deeply incised decorations; most often used on large screens made in China for export to the West in the late 17th and early 18th centuries.

Dado paneling—paneling between floor and dado railing (see below).

Dado railing—molding running around room at approximately waist height.

Damask—a fabric with a reversible, double-faced weave system, in which the pattern is created by the warps and wefts.

Delftware—tin-glazed earthenware named for the Dutch city of Delft, which was the center of its production in the 17th century; the term delftware is also applied to similar ware made in England.

Denticulation—decorative motif in which small, rectangular, teeth-like blocks (dentils) are arranged in a series under a cornice (see above).

Dower chest—box or trunk designed to contain a bride's dowry.

Embrasure—opening for a door, window, etc., usually with the sides slanted so it is wider on the inside.

Etagère—set of open shelves that can be free-standing, part of another piece of furniture, or built into a wall; generally used for display purposes.

Faïence ware—derived from a French term for tin-glazed earthenware.

Finial—a decorative knob applied as an ornamental element to architecture, furniture, or the covers of vessels made in ceramic, silver, etc.

These items, drawn from the American miniature rooms, are pictured in their actual sizes based on a scale of one inch to a foot. The desk and accessories, desk chair, and sewing table are from Room A-25; the newspaper stand from A-15; the steam engine and antique doll from A-33; and the rug from A-16.

Fretwork—carved geometrical patterns of intersecting straight lines, at right or oblique angles, repeated to form a band, pierced or in relief.

Gate-leg table—a type of drop-leaf table, the leaves of which are supported by legs hinged to a central support.

Girandole—term used variously for free-standing candelabra or wall sconces of varying media and complexity, whose name was derived from the Italian *girandola,* a kind of revolving firework.

Gobelins manufactory—the most important Parisian manufactory of the late 17th and 18th centuries; created in 1663 by Louis XIV's minister of finance J. B. Colbert (1619-1683) to provide splendid furnishings in all media (most notably wall-hangings) for the king's residences.

Grotesque—complex, fanciful decorative compositions of loosely connected motifs that can include human and fantastic figures, plants, and animals.

Inlay—decorative technique in which a pattern is created with different colored woods or materials, such as ivory, mother-of-pearl or metal, set flush into a solid background panel (usually wood); replaced for the most part by marquetry (see below) in the 17th century.

Jacquard—a loom apparatus invented by J. M. Jacquard (1752-1834) which, through a mechanism controlled by perforated cards, is capable of producing complicated figural patterns.

Japanning—any of various methods used to imitate Oriental lacquer in Europe and North America where the resin of the lac-tree, *rhus vernicifera,* was not available; often involves the application to wood of many layers of a compound of seedlac or shellac dissolved in spirits of wine and usually colored black.

Jasperware—fine-grained, hard, slightly translucent stoneware capable of being stained a variety of colors, perfected by the Wedgwood factory (see below) in 1775.

Joined chair—chair of which the component parts are fitted together with mortise and tenon joints (in which the protruding end, or tenon, is inserted into a socket, or mortise).

Joiner—woodworker, furniture maker.

Khmer—Cambodian empire which was established in the 6th century, whose highly developed civilization reached its apogee in the 12th century.

Lacquer—waterproof varnish of Oriental origin; true Chinese or Japanese lacquer was created by a long process using the gum of the lac-tree, *rhus vernicifera,* not available in Europe or North America (see also *japanning* above).

Latticework—diagonally constructed crossmembers, often used in chair backs and table supports; an openwork fret (see *fretwork* above).

Marquetry—decorative veneer of shaped pieces of colored woods and such materials as bone, ivory, mother-of-pearl or metal, applied to the carcass (see above) of furniture to form patterned decorations; first practiced in Germany and the Low Countries and introduced to France and England in the 17th century.

Meridienne sofa—an Empire and Restoration design in which one end is higher than the other.

Oculus—an architectural element resembling an eye, such as a round opening in a dome.

Ormolu—decorative objects such as furniture mounts made of cast, chased, and fire-gilt bronze.

Pedestal table—round- or square-top table supported on a central column or pier.

Pembroke table—elegant, drop-leaf table supported by four legs and with hinged leaves on the sides; dating from the mid-18th century, it was most likely named after the Countess of Pembroke (1737-1831).

Pilaster—an architectural element consisting of a shallow pier or rectangular column, attached to a wall, cupboard, or cabinet front.

Pole screen—small fire-screen, consisting of a square-, oval- or shield-shaped panel fixed to an upright pole resting on tripod legs.

Press—Old English term for a cupboard used to store clothes, books, linen, etc., as in clothes-press, linen-press.

Press cupboard—specific term for a 16th- or 17th-century piece of furniture with doors enclosing a large compartment below and two smaller compartments above.

Prie-dieu—a piece of furniture often comprised of a low-seated chair with a high back and padded top, upon which one can kneel to pray.

Savonnerie carpet manufactory—the most important European factory of fine knotted-pile carpets; founded in France in 1627 by Louis XIII, it merged with the Gobelins manufactory (see above) in 1825.

Sconce—wall light consisting of one or more bracket candlesticks and usually a polished, reflective back plate (often a mirror after the 17th century).

Scroll—ornamental form consisting of a spiral line, so-named because it resembles a roll of parchment or paper.

Secretary—desk or writing table, usually mounted on a stand or chest of drawers and having a fall front.

Settee—seat with back and arms designed for two or more people.

Settle—bench with back and arms, used especially in farmhouses and taverns from medieval times to the early 20th century.

Sideboard—a side table used for serving, invented in the early 1760s by the English architect and furniture designer Robert Adam (1728-1792).

Soffit—the underside of an overhead architectural element; more specifically, the underside of an arch, lintel, etc.

Spindle—slender, turned, etc. used in balusters, chair backs, etc.

Splat—central, vertical member of a chair back, between the seat and top-rail, often shaped or pierced.

Split-turned ornament—small, turned (chiseled on a lathe) wood balusters or spindles (see above) split vertically and applied to furniture as relief decoration; much in use until about 1700.

Sprigged—decorated with a design of twigs or other small foliage forms.

Staffordshire pottery—wares produced by a large group of English ceramic factories located in the Staffordshire region, which have been in operation from the 17th century to the present; products are mainly lead- or salt-glazed (never tin-glazed) earthenware and stoneware; from the 19th century on, the chief products were simple household wares and statuettes.

Strapwork—three-dimensional (carved, molded, or hammered) surface ornament, resembling interwoven leather straps.

Stucco—mixture of sand and a bonding agent (lime or cement) applied to a wall as a protective or decorative covering.

Swag—draped cloth ornament tied with ribbons and suspended at one or both ends in a loop; rendered in wood or composition (see above), it was used as a decorative element, particularly in the 18th century.

Tambour—roll front made of narrow wooden strips attached with glue to a canvas backing, used for desks, cupboard doors, etc.

Tester—canopy, usually of carved wood and supported by four corner posts, covering the whole area of a bed; a half-tester was one that was cantilevered from the head posts and covered about one-third of the bed.

Torchère—portable stand for a candle or lamp; generally like a tall table with a small top, but also can be figural.

Tracery—architectural ornamental work of interlacing lines, usually found in the head of a Gothic window.

Trestle-base table—supported by two or more inverted T- or Y-shapes braced by a horizontal beam.

Veneer—thin sheets of fine wood applied to the carcass (see above) of furniture (made of coarser wood), for a decorative effect.

Wainscot—planking used to panel rooms as well as to construct chairs.

Wedgwood ceramics manufactory—famous establishment of Englishman Josiah Wedgwood (1730-1795), which from the 1760s to the present has produced ceramic wares mainly in the Neoclassical style.

Whiting—powdered chalk used in the production of paints.

Windsor chair—comfortable country piece, originating in England and very popular in America; the seat is solid, shaped wood, into which the legs and spindles (see above) are doweled.

Wing chair—upholstered chair with padded arms and a high back with sides or wings, originally intended to protect the sitter from drafts.